Jazz in Love

Other Titles by Neesha Meminger

shine, coconut moon

Jazz in Love

Neesha Meminger

Ignite

Ignite Books, New York

Ignite Books, NY

For information about this title, please contact info@ignite-books.com
Cover design by Sherin Nicole
Cover photograph © Huchen Lu / iPandastudio / iStockphoto Images
Author photograph © Craig Blankenhorn
The text for this book is set in Georgia
10 9 8 7 6 5 4 3 2 1
Meminger, Neesha
Jazz in Love / Neesha Dosanjh Meminger.--1st ed.
Summary: When her mother launches the Guided Dating Plan
to find Jazz the perfect, suitable, pre-screened Indian mate,
Jazz realizes she must act fast to find a way to follow her own
heart and stay in the good graces of her parents.
Library of Congress Control Number 2010917279
ISBN 978-0-983-1583-0-1 (paperback)
ISBN 978-0-983-1583-1-8 (eBook)

To the seventeen-year-old in all of us—still there—just listen.

~ ✻ ~

And, of course, as ever, to Satya and Laini.

The hunger for love is much more difficult to remove than the hunger for bread.
~ Mother Theresa

Love makes your soul crawl out from its hiding place.
~ Zora Neale Hurston

Before I met my husband, I'd never fallen in love. I'd stepped in it a few times.
~ Rita Rudner

Romance is dead – it was acquired in a hostile takeover by Hallmark and Disney, homogenized, and sold off piece by piece.
~ Lisa Simpson, *The Simpsons*

~ ❋ ~

Acknowledgments

This book would not have been possible without the warmth and unmitigated support of the author community—including YA and MG authors, the authors-of-colour who are my comrades in the struggle for accurate representation, passionate book bloggers and reviewers (Tarie, Edi, Doret, Susan, Ari, Colleen—I'm looking at you!), and the many teachers and librarians who wholeheartedly support diversity in books for young people. Even with the heartaches, disappointments, dips and summits of this process, this community is the one shining gem I would never trade for anything.

I would like to extend a special, heartfelt thank you to Olugbemisola Rhuday-Perkovich, who is always ready to lend her warmth, generosity of spirit, humour and hugs when they are most needed, and for knowing what I mean every time I say, "Know what I mean?"; The Rejectionist, who is an ardent ally for marginalized voices and a fellow lover of great food; Sherin Nicole for jumping in during the final hour and cleaning things up; Cynthea Liu and Zetta Elliott for being trailblazers and encouraging me to press on; and to the numerous friends and supporters who've lent their energies and insights as I navigated these choppy, unpredictable waters.

I am deeply grateful for the keen insight and sharp editing skills of Sarah Cloots. Thank you, Sarah, for being such an enthusiastic supporter of Jazz and her friends!

Thank you, also, to the young adults at *SAYA!* in Queens, NY, for reminding me that seventeen is seventeen, whether it was then, or now; in Toronto, Vancouver, Yuba City, Atlanta, London, or New York City. Though a lot of things change, the struggle to express and embrace oneself fully in the face of incessant social, political, economic, cultural and familial restrictions remains steadfast.

I would be completely remiss if I did not extend my sincerest gratitude to the Dhatts for allowing me to pepper my book with their family name. Kinder, especially, who in no way resembles the character of Auntie Kinder, but whose name and accent (when I first met her) were the inspiration for this feisty character I've grown to love. And to the Birk girls—who might find bits and pieces of themselves in the Reda-Rodriguez sisters.

Most importantly, thank you from the bottom of my heart, to my partner-in-crime, Hollis, who has weathered the tears and breakdowns that no one else sees; and my crazy, wonderful, amazing kids—the greatest motivators in my life.

Highest honor must go, as always, to the ancestors and the Larger Life Force that runs through us all.

Chapter 1

"My *mom's making me* pick out a husband."

Cindy Reda-Rodriguez, my best friend since kindergarten, stopped tying her shoelaces and stared at me. "A *what?*"

I walked through the library doors. "Okay, maybe not a husband, *per se*," I said, heading toward the cluster of tables near the back. "But they want me to start looking for . . . you know—a life partner," I said miserably.

"You just turned seventeen!" she shrieked.

Half the kids in the library turned around.

"Sorry," Cindy mumbled, waving away the curious stares. She leaned in and whispered, "*Seriously?*"

Miss Fry, the Physical Health and Sciences teacher Cindy and I had in freshman year, poked her head around one of the aisles. "Keep it down."

When she saw it was us, the stern look on her face morphed into a bright smile. "Oh, hello, girls!"

We smiled and said hi, then walked to an empty table that was far enough away from too many eager ears, but still one where we could keep an eye on who came and went. Jeeves had said he might join us.

Me, Cindy, and Jeevan "Jeeves" Sahota were all in the Future Stars and Leaders (FSL) Program at Maple Ridge High, New York.

"Over the holidays, someone my mom knows from The Community saw me hugging Jeeves good-bye and now she and my dad think they need to kick the Find Jazz A Suitable Partner Before She Finds A Very *Unsuitable* One NOW Plan into overdrive."

"Oh, is that all?" Cindy said, looking relieved. "You and Jeeves have known each other since we were kids, your moms know each other . . . just explain that it was nothing."

"No way. You know I can't, Cin. My parents don't understand the concept of boys and girls hugging *platonically*. They go ballistic if there's any physical contact at all. I can't tell her it was him."

"But, he's . . . *Jeeves*."

"That means nothing. She might forbid me to ever see him again," I said.

Cindy shook her head. "I doubt she'd do that, Jazz. He's, like, one of our best friends."

"One of our best friends who's a *guy*. Even if my mom knows nothing is going on, it *looks* bad if anyone from The Community ever saw me with a guy who's not related to me by blood." I sighed. As much as Cindy sort of understood what the deal was with my life, there were some things she just didn't get.

I flipped through my calculus textbook and glanced at Cindy out of the corner of my eye. She had her trying-to-understand face on.

"She said that since I was starting to 'show interest in boys,'" I whispered, "she would ask the 'family matchmakers' to send pictures for me to choose from."

Cindy's eyes widened. "No. *Way.*"

Her disbelief made me feel even worse. "She calls it 'guided dating.' Starting this Saturday, I am allowed to have *zero* contact with the opposite sex unless he's slated to be my future spouse."

Cindy shook her head. "Wow. I hope there are a lot of cute guys in those pictures."

Miss Fry walked by us on her way out. "Nice to see you, girls." Teachers loved us. They all knew the kids from the FSL program. It was almost like we were academic rock stars.

We waved as she headed toward the double library doors. And there, just outside the doors, walking next to a couple of bonehead jocks, was the absolute *epitome* of gorgeosity.

I looked at Cindy. "Who. Is. *That?*"

She grinned. "That is serious new hottie extraordinaire, Tyler R. His last name is, like, twenty-seven letters long, so everyone just calls him Tyler R." She looked toward the doors, where the group of guys had stopped and congregated, and fanned her face.

I looked over too, along with several other girls from around the tables, and Tyler R. gave us this sort of lop-sided smile through the glass doors.

"He's Indian!" I said, sudden hope soaring in my chest.

"I heard from Mandy Morgan, who heard from Bethany McCourt, that he's from Trinidad, and he just transferred here this semester from Wendell Academy."

"Oh." Crash landing on the soaring hope. My parents had very clear rules for what the term "Indian" encompassed. Apparently, the person being appraised had to have been born in India, or their parents or grandparents had to have been born in India. In that order. And going as far back as the grandparents was pushing it—even with the grandparents being born in India, things could get iffy. It was all about preserving Culture and Tradition—two things my parents were *very* big on. And the more I thought about it, the more it seemed that, in my parents' grand scheme of things, "India" didn't even include other parts of India. Apparently, the boundaries of India never strayed far from Punjab.

I sighed and looked back at the hunk of gorgeosity just outside the glass double doors. Was it me, or did his eyes rest just a smidgen longer on me than they had on the other girls? I shook my head. Couldn't be.

"O.M.G. He totally knows how hot he is," I said, my stomach knotting up. He looked like he'd walked straight off the cover of one of the romance novels I kept stuffed under my pillow.

"Of *course* he does," Cindy said. "Any girl in the vicinity would give either of her noonies to be that T-shirt stretched across his abs."

I watched him walk away, with his crew of boneheads, after exchanging flirty smiles with several of the girls in the hall, and swallowed the familiar lump in my throat—the one reminding me that those kinds of shared, secret smiles were simply not in the cards for girls like me.

Saturday morning, I woke up to a spread of glossy prints on our coffee table.

My mom smiled pleasantly and pointed a long finger to a spot on the loveseat. "Sit," she commanded.

My dad was snoring on the sofa. He worked the late afternoon shift at a medical supplies factory, even on Saturdays, and was trying to sneak in a few more hours of sleep.

"Pick out some photos, Jassy."

"It's Jazz. Mom, seriously. Can you *please* call me Jazz?"

She gave me a look. "I am not Cindy, or one of your friends. You are my Jassy. That's it." She turned back to the task at hand. "There is a brief biography of each boy on the back of his photo. Put aside the ones you want to know more about."

I looked at the images of strangers and, for a moment, thought I might hurl.

My mom sat down next to me. "It's okay, *beta*," she said, stroking my back. "This is a big decision, I know, but you take your time, *heh-na*? You'll meet the boy, spend some time together, and Daddy and I will be right by your side the whole time, *accha*?"

Accha = okay. This is so not accha.

"Go ahead, now. Look through," she said, getting up and heading to the kitchen.

I picked up a picture of a not-so-bad-looking face and turned it over: ONKAR MANN. 5' 3". 140 LBS.

Lovely.

My mom opened the refrigerator. "Jassy," she called, after groping around for several minutes. "Don't forget to call your Kinder Auntie back later—she called this morning."

"Can't I call her now?" I asked, flipping over another picture.

"Absolutely not," she said, shutting the fridge door and sticking her head out to glare at me. "Just give them a chance, Jassy. They can't *all* be defective."

Wrong. "What if I end up with someone like Mr. Auntie Kinder?"

Auntie Kinder—the term *she* preferred (rather than "Kinder Auntie," which was my parents' version. The "uncle" or "auntie" came after the person's name in Indian-parent-lingo)—who was not related to me by blood, and her eleven-year-old daughter, Pammi, had lived in our basement for a few years after Auntie Kinder left her husband and "fled" England, according to my mom. The ex-husband had apparently mistaken Auntie Kinder for a punching bag.

The glare faded from her eyes and she rushed over to sit next to me again. "Oh, Jassy, *beta*," she said, taking my hand in hers. "Your father and I would never allow that. We would interview the boy and the family very carefully, and you would spend as much time as you like getting to know him before anyone made any commitments. Remember, you won't have to get married right away. Kinder's parents rushed her marriage because. . . ." Her eyes flitted away for a moment before she stretched a smile across her face and continued. "Never mind. We would take our time."

I stared at the array of snapshots. I pointed to each photo in turn. "Big honker . . . Looks like an axe murderer" (gasp from my mom) ". . . *He's* about to orbit the earth with those ears. . . ."

She sighed. "*Hiyo Rubba*, Jassy. At some point you will have to be more open minded."

My eyes almost popped out of my head. "Open minded? Me? *Me?*"

She sucked her teeth in annoyance. "Of course, *you*. These are all fine young men from lovely family backgrounds. And you cannot find a single one to interest you."

"I just turned seventeen."

She pointed to the spread of smiling glossies in front of me. "I was almost married at your age. You have no idea how lucky you are to have modern parents, Jassy. We are letting *you* pick. Completely your choice."

"What about meeting someone on my own, falling in love—"

"Nonsense," she interrupted, pressing her lips together. Then, in a gentler tone, "You don't have to go through all that nonsense. You have perfectly good, pre-screened candidates here. And if none of these suits your picky palate, then there are plenty more where they came from."

I folded my arms across my chest and sulked.

She stared at me quietly for several minutes. Finally she said, "Fine," in a too-loud voice.

I looked at her suspiciously. My mother agreeing with me was never a good sign.

She gathered all the pictures together with a wide sweeping motion of her arms. "No photos on the coffee table, then," she said, stacking them together in piles.

"Huh?"

She held one finger up and looked intently at me. "But you must meet this fellow from Canada your Mindo Auntie told me all about."

See?

"He is being wooed by the Ivies here in America, this young man. Very bright future ahead of him . . . podiatry, I think, *heh-na?*" She looked over her shoulder at my dad's sleeping form for confirmation.

After no response, she nodded. "Yes, podiatry," she said, satisfied.

"A geek," I said miserably.

She leaned back, mouth dropping open in amazement. "What geek? Isn't that how others in your school refer to you and Cindy and Jeevan, and all of the other bright FSL students?"

"We are FSL," I clarified. "Therefore, we are *cool* geeks. We are a different *brand* of geekiness. We are geek *chic*."

She waved away my words and tapped the edges of each stack of photographs, making sure they were in perfect rectangular alignment.

I sighed. "So . . . I'll call Auntie Kinder now," I said, heaving myself up. "Then I have to *study*." Big emphasis on the "study" part—it had been my escape hatch since I was a kid.

My mom nodded, but pressed her lips together again, keeping her eyes trained on the photos she was now separating into envelopes. "You will meet this fellow," she repeated as I climbed the stairs to my room. "I have a feeling about him. I think he'll be a perfect match for you."

I sent up a silent prayer to whatever gods were on duty to please make Mr. Canadian Podiatrist-in-Training look like new hottie, Tyler R.

I thought things couldn't possibly get any worse than having my parents "guide" my dating and possibly pick out my future life partner. But of course, just when you think things can't possibly get worse. . . .

Chapter 2

On Sunday, Auntie Kinder's eleven-year-old daughter, Pammi, came over to hang out for a few hours while Auntie Kinder had her weekly "me time."

My dad was out running errands and getting the car tuned up, and my mom was upstairs henna-ing her hair. I was watching some PG-rated teen movie with Pammi when the doorbell rang.

When I looked through the peephole, all I could see was a pair of super-hairy forearms crossed at the chest. "Who is it?" I called through the closed door.

"I am here for Kinder and Parminder Dhillon."

Even from the sofa, with the TV on, Pammi heard the voice and blanched. She rushed over to sneak a peek through the peephole and shrank back into the corner behind the door.

"Just a minute," I said to the hairy forearms. I motioned Pammi upstairs and mouthed, "Get my mom." Then I gulped and opened the door carefully, ready to slam it shut if needed.

"Who are you?" he commanded immediately.

For a minute, I couldn't remember my own name.

British accent. Tall, hairy dude. So this was the infamous Mr. Auntie Kinder.

I narrowed my eyes at him. "I'm sorry," I said, standing taller. "But who are *you*? You rang *my* doorbell."

He scowled. "Where is your father?"

Just then, my mom scrambled down the stairs with a plastic thingy wrapped around her head. "What is it, Jassy?"

I kept the door firmly where it was, in case this dude had any funny ideas.

My mom stopped abruptly by my side. "Oh—!"

He held his hands in front of him, prayer style, in greeting. "Sat sri akal, *behenji*," he said, in the same commanding tone. "I've come to retrieve my wife and daughter."

Retrieve?

"I'm sorry," my mom said, casually reaching across me for the door. She gently shoved me back and away. "Your wife is not here."

She made no reference to Pammi at all.

He bent his head into the house to look around. "*Behenji*," he said, when he was satisfied that no one else was there. "I know she is staying here. Family and friends have told me you have been hiding them. You *must* return them to me, or I will be forced to take extreme measures."

My mom closed the door further and blocked him from my view completely. "We are not *hiding* anyone, *bhaji*. I have told you once that your wife is not here. Are you calling me a liar? She and Pammi no longer live with us. Indeed, they did years back, but no more. I do not know where she is right now."

I looked at her, impressed. I was sure no other woman could wear a plastic head-wrap thingy and still sound as authoritative as my mom did right then.

"This is my and my *husband's* house, *bhaji*," she said.

I suddenly recalled her telling me once that some men only took the word of other men seriously—apparently, this was one of those men, hence her great emphasis on the word "husband."

"If you choose to harass us further," she continued, "we shall be forced to resort to extreme measures of our own."

There were a few minutes of complete, tense silence as my mom and Big, Burly, Bearded Dude—former Mr. Auntie Kinder—faced off against each other.

I stood with my entire body coiled, waiting, and I'm sure Pammi was totally freaking upstairs. If he barged in or something, and tried to drag Pammi away, he'd have to fight me and my mom first.

Finally, he stepped back. "If I find out you are hiding my family, I will have no choice." And then he stalked away.

Mom shut the door quickly and locked it. I turned and saw Pammi slowly inching down the stairs.

My mom closed her eyes for a moment like she was trying to compose herself, then reached to pull me and Pammi, who ran the rest of the way down, into her arms.

Pammi began to tremble and sob.

I exploded. "Can you believe that guy?!"

My mom was silent as she held us and gently stroked Pammi's back.

"What does he mean, '*You must return them to me*'?! Like they have tags saying, 'Property of Mr. Auntie Kinder. If found please return to owner'. . . ?"

My mom released me. "Jassy, *beta*, call Kinder's cell phone. Tell her to come as soon as possible—but you must warn her to be cautious."

I grabbed the house phone and punched in Auntie Kinder's cell number, getting her voice mail. "Auntie Kinder, you have to come quick. Mr. . . your ex-husband was just here."

Exactly thirteen seconds later, she called back to say she was on her way. And in about nine minutes flat, she screeched into the driveway. So much for being cautious.

I opened the door just in time for her to swoosh past me to Pammi. Auntie Kinder folded Pammi into her arms, then held her out at arm's length. She took Pammi's face and turned it from side to side. "What did he say, Deesh?" she asked my mom.

"He was looking for you. Pammi, too, but he's after you." She shook her head, then muttered, "You are, apparently, still 'his.'"

"Ooohh, that man!" Auntie Kinder snarled. She slammed a fist into her other hand and paced the kitchen floor once she was sure that Pammi was okay. "Did he say anything about how long he's here?"

Mom shook her head. "No. But clearly you and Pammi should stay away from here for some time. At least until we find out for certain how long he is here. I'll ask around in the community."

Auntie Kinder stopped pacing and stared out the kitchen window, into our back-yard. "That son of a—"

"Kinder, take Pammi home," my mom said quickly. "He doesn't know where you live—it's good you took those precautions with the post-office box and such."

Auntie Kinder nodded. "Did he see you, Pams?"

Pammi drew a shaky breath. "Would I still be here if he saw me?"

"Oh, darling. . . ." Auntie Kinder's eyes filled as she crushed Pammi to her chest again. "Let's go home."

That night, as I tried to concentrate on my homework, all I could see was a pair of burly forearms and hairy-knuckled fists. I paced back and forth in my room for several minutes before picking up the phone.

Pammi answered. "Hey, Pams, it's Jazz."

"Hi, Jazz." She sounded like a little kid, even younger than eleven.

"How you doing?"

"I'm okay," she mumbled. "A little better. My mom started calling around as soon as we got home, and found out from some family in England that he's only here on a stopover. So he should be on his way back there tomorrow morning."

"Oh, thank *God* . . . what a relief!"

I heard Auntie Kinder in the background, then Pammi yelling away from the phone, "It's Jazz!"

Auntie Kinder came on. "Hello, darling." She sounded nothing like the bubbly, cheerful Auntie Kinder I'd always known, but she seemed better than earlier.

"Heard Pammi's dad is on his way back to where he came from tomorrow."

"Indeed," she said. "But the fact that he sought us out while he was here is troubling." There was a pause where I could hear some muffled back and forth with Pammi. "I'll hand you back to Pammi in a second, Jazz," she said, coming back on. "But I wanted to ask if you could stay with her on Thursday nights for a little while? I'd signed up for a course that I've already paid for."

"I think it's okay. I'll check with my mom."

"I've already checked with Deesh. She's fine with it, as long as your school-work doesn't suffer."

"Okay, so it's cool then," I said happily. I loved hanging out with Auntie Kinder and Pammi.

"Lovely!" She sounded relieved.

I wanted to take her mind off her own, way serious, problems. So I brought up my own. "So . . . um, my mom just made me stare at pictures of fine, eligible, pre-screened young men."

"Did you find your soul mate, then?" she asked with an almost-laugh. Success!

"It's *not* funny. What if they find someone like—" I caught myself right before I said "your ex-husband."

"No, it isn't," she said more seriously. "Oh, darling, your mother and father are reasonable people." She paused for a moment, before continuing. "Jazz. My parents were in a rush to marry me off because they caught me, erm . . . kissing a boy when I was quite young."

I almost dropped the phone. Auntie Kinder—"caught" with a boy? I cleared my throat and said as casually as I could, "What do you mean?"

She lowered her voice. "Well, er . . . they caught a class fellow and I being, er, rather affectionate in a car, and . . . well, let's just say they pressed the gas pedal on marrying me off to a nice, 'more suitable' boy."

Suddenly, a bunch of questions tumbled out before I could stop them. "Who was the boy? What were you guys doing? Wait, scratch that, I don't want to know. How did they catch you? How long had you and him—"

She raised her voice slightly. "Not important. What *is* important is that *you* can talk to your parents about your feelings."

Crud. I guess, understandably, she was in no mood for "girl talk" tonight. I let it go for now, but swore to find out more about Auntie Kinder's premarital make-out history (!!).

"Come on," I said glumly, "do you really believe my parents could be reasonable?"

"Course I do," she said. "After all, they let me and Pammi stay in your basement for over a year without paying a single penny in rent."

"True. But they're different when it comes to me."

"We're all different when it comes to our own children, love. Give them a chance. You might be surprised."

"Highly doubt it. Besides, I may already have found the love of my life."

"'Zat so?" There was amusement in her voice. Very annoying.

"*Yes,*" I said, maybe a tad more forcefully than necessary. "He's new, and he's *stunning.*"

"Well," she said, still sounding annoyingly amused. "I suppose you've got a bit of a dilemma on your hands, then."

After wondering why some British people put an "r" at the end of words like "dilemma" and "America," I hung up the phone and thought long and hard about Auntie Kinder's marriage to a hairy-fisted psycho. I wondered how her parents had found the former Mr. AK. Did they have smiling snapshots of boys to choose from? Were they planning to one day have Auntie Kinder sit at a coffee table and pick her life partner?

What would have happened if they had never discovered her making out with that guy in the car? What would've happened if she had married *him,* instead—someone *she* had picked? Maybe her guy-radar was better tuned than her parents', but they were just too stuck in old-crotchety-parent-ness to see it.

Leaving me alone to ponder such things was obviously dangerous, because that's when I came up with the beginnings of The Plan—a series of events that would change Auntie Kinder's life . . . and mine, forever.

Chapter 3

I was outlining The Plan in my notebook as Cindy chomped on an apple next to me in the cafeteria during lunch.

> *1) Find out about guy from A.K.'s past. Was he the love of her life? Where is he now? Is he a bum on the streets? Is he a jerk like her ex-husband? Or is he Mr. Dream Dude, like Tyler R.?*
>
> *2) If aforementioned Guy From Past is the latter, figure out how to get said guy back together with A.K—*

And then Tyler R. walked in.

"Omigosh, it's *Tyler R.*," Cindy breathed, nudging me with her elbow. The letter "K" extended itself across half the page as I jerked my head up.

Sure enough, there was Tyler R., gliding down the center of the cafeteria.

Cindy screwed her face up. "*Yich.* Would you look at those two? It's, like, thirty degrees out and they're wearing string bikinis. Can somebody please tell them it's *January* in upstate New York?"

"They're not wearing string bikinis, Cin," I said, in a lame effort to defend Priya and Zahra.

Leave it to Cindy. I probably would've thought it, especially with Priya's frilly pink thong showing above the waistline of her jeans, but I wouldn't have said it out *loud.* You know, brown solidarity and all. They might be bindi-bos (bindis slash bimbos), but it's in the Brown Solidarity Handbook: *Thou shalt not publicly denounce thine brown brethren and sistren. Even the bindi-bos.*

I looked back at Tyler R. His skin was a goldish-brown, like the fossilized amber amulets that Auntie Kinder sometimes wore. I was *so* swooning.

Even though Cindy'd heard he'd gone to Wendell Academy, I heard some of the bindi-bos whispering that he came straight out of juvie hall, where he spent all summer doing time for selling drugs and other offenses. Not that the bindi-bos' word was gospel or anything.

I looked down for a moment to catch my breath. When I looked back up, I slammed into his gaze.

Cindy grabbed my elbow. "*Omigosh*! He was *totally* checking you out."

"I don't think so. . . ." I said. "He didn't break a smile or anything."

She rolled her eyes. "He's *intense*, Jazz. That's how you know he's for *real*."

Maybe. But holy frack! *Tyler R!!!!!* Mrs. Tyler R. Mrs. Jazz R. Popular, athletic, hawt, Tyler R. and . . . *me*. Could it possibly be that he was checking me out? But no—no one from the "regular" classes ever mixed with the FSL kids. Still . . . could it be?

For the rest of the afternoon, I couldn't focus on a *thing*. Visions of Tyler R. sailed through my head. When he'd looked at me in the cafeteria, it had seemed like he was peering down into a well, seeing every little secret I kept tucked away from the world.

When I got home from school, I found my dad already zonked out on the couch. His shifts started around four-thirty or so, and went till past midnight. Most of the other brown kids around us had parents who were doctors, engineers, or lawyers. Mine both worked in factories, but saved every last cent so we could live in a nice house, in a nice neighborhood, so that I could go to a good school. Education, specifically mine, was apparently going to emancipate our whole family.

I walked up the stairs to my room, and stuck my head out to listen to my dad's snoring for a minute before pulling out my latest romance novel. If my parents ever got a glimpse of one of those book covers—ample-bosom cleavage and hard, bronzed pecs galore—they would immediately book me a one way ticket to India to straighten me out. No, thank you. Romance novels got smuggled into my house with secret-agent, espionage-level security. And then Cindy and I dog-eared the pages with the dirty parts and swapped books.

When I was sure the coast was clear, I cozied into my overstuffed armchair and cracked open *Love's Wayward Journey*. As I read, my mind created forbidden, very UN-good-Indian-girl images with me and Tyler R. in the starring roles. We were sailing the high seas, me in my too-tight-around-the-boobs dress and him in his button-down, white, pirate-like shirt. It was one of those old-fashioned historical novels that I loved.

Those British in the old days did exactly what we did in India—dowries and arranged marriages and no kissing or affection in public. I always wondered how they managed to weasel out of it, while we still hung on.

But, of course, what I *should* have been wondering about was that old saying, "Be careful what you wish for. . . ."

That Thursday, I went to Auntie Kinder's after school to watch Pammi. Except Pammi hadn't come home from school yet and Auntie Kinder's class had been cancelled.

I decided this was a perfect opportunity to put my plan in motion. "So . . . what was his name?" I asked.

"Whose name?" she said, dumping a load of clean clothes between us on the rug.

"The guy you got caught making out with."

"Oh, for Heaven's sake, Jazz."

"You know me," I said with a grin. "My middle name is Bug when I want to know something."

She put her hands on her hips and pursed her lips. "Very true," she conceded. "If I tell you, you must *promise* to drop it, all right?"

I held up a pinky. "Pinky swear."

She sat down cross-legged on the other side of the clothing mound and rolled up a pair of Pammi's socks. "Babaloo."

"Babaloo?" I asked incredulously.

She gave me a look of utter exasperation. "I'll have you know, little miss, that Babaloo is a very special term of endearment among us Punjabis. Ask your mother."

Was that a note of defensiveness I detected? "Okay, so . . . Babaloo."

She shook out a pair of jeans. "Yes. Babaloo." Somehow, coming from her, it sounded like the most dignified, desirable name on the planet for a guy.

"I thought he was the love of my life. I used to think we'd marry each other . . . we'd talked about it, in fact. We'd known one another since we were children. . . ." She slowly ran a hand down the length of the jeans to smooth out any wrinkles. "We both knew our parents would never approve. . . ."

A bitter edge crept into her voice. "Sikhism is supposed to be caste-less. That was the whole point of separating from Hinduism . . . but obviously, not everyone adheres to those ideals."

I picked up a T-shirt as carefully as I could, not wanting to break the spell, and started folding with great precision.

But then, all at once, she seemed to snap out of the memory. "But all of that is water under the bridge. He became some sort of doctor—a psychologist, I believe. I've heard he's done quite well for himself in the U.K. We lost touch completely, after I got married."

I tried to think of ways to bring the conversation back.

But after a brief silence, Auntie Kinder looked up and straight into my eyes. "There you have it. Now, drop it, Jazz."

The tone of her voice left no question: this matter was sealed shut.

I nodded, though I really had no intention of dropping it. It just felt too . . . *important.* Everything she *didn't* say was screaming to me that this matter was *not* sealed shut.

Chapter 4

I won't say it never occurred to me that if I could *somehow* get Auntie Kinder and the former love-of-her-life back together, not only would I be helping her, but I also might be able to prove to my parents that it could work—that meeting someone and falling in love was a completely viable path to marriage.

I asked Pammi a few innocuous questions about where she grew up in London and if she knew where Auntie Kinder grew up—like, where did her grandparents live and stuff. That info, combined with some savvy Googling (Useful School-Taught Skill # 3: Prying into people's lives using Internet search engines), and the fact that Babaloo is a nickname that most folks grew out of, but one person, apparently, hung on to—gave me some clues on where to start my investigation.

That weekend was a long one to celebrate Martin Luther King, Jr. Day, so I had an extra day to begin my trawling venture on the interwebs. I tried searching for "Babaloo psychologist England," which brought up a few links, mainly for a blogger named Babalu, with a "u". Still, I clicked on all the ones that came up. The last one had a link to a *Doctor* Babaloo who still lived in the U.K., and had a wildly successful TV show where he gave advice and therapy to mostly "Asian" families. I moved closer to the screen as my pulse ratcheted up just a tiny notch.

I watched several clips on YouTube, and learned that "Asian" in the U.K. did not mean what I was used to it meaning here in the U. S. of A—it meant brown people there, apparently. Dr. Babaloo had all kinds of brown people on, not all from India— some were from Bangladesh, Pakistan, Sri Lanka, and other places I'd never even heard of. He called it "Indians from the *diaspora*." There were places like Bhutan (which, contrary to what I first thought when I heard it, is *not* a hip-hop group out of Brooklyn, New York) and Surinam. Sometimes he devoted a whole show to Indians from the Caribbean (which I paid especially close attention to because of one Tyler R.).

Encouraged, I clicked over to his official site. His biography said that Dr. Babaloo was divorced, with a grown daughter who had her own segment on his show. Now, you'd probably expect something like a cross between Deepak Chopra and Dr. Phil, but no. His headshot showed an Indian George Clooney, only with frizzy hair that grew out, in a kind of Indi-fro donut thingy (he had a shiny bald spot smack center on the top of his head).

I went back to Google and tried the search terms, "Dr. Babaloo dating history" and voilá! I got something like ninety thousand listings. I clicked on the first few.

Apparently, Dr. Babaloo was a busy guy. He had dated a huge list of celebrity hotties, including one of the girls from the British girl band, The Hissin' Kittens. Those were the ones who gyrated their pelvises two inches from the camera, using a few strings to cover their crucials. More specifically, he'd dated Viper Kitten—the one with the three pigtails, two on the sides and one directly above where a bindi usually goes, giving her a sort of fairy/unicorn-ish appearance.

One YouTube interview, in particular, had me up way past when my parents were happily snoring away. A fan of Dr. Babaloo's had uploaded an interview of his with Anjula Reddy, host of *In the Spotlight* in London:

Anjula Reddy: *Good afternoon, and thank you for joining us for another hour of* In the Spotlight. *Today, we're chatting with Dr. Babaloo, author of several self-help books for parents of Asian teens and host of his own popular daytime talk show.*

Dr. Babaloo, you live an unconventional lifestyle, far removed from the lives of most Asian families in the U.K. How can you offer sound advice to the average Asian parent when you're not really connected to those day-to-day issues?

Dr. Babaloo (smiling and leaning forward with the fingertips on both hands together like a teepee): *Well, Anjula* [he said "Anjular"], *I didn't always live this "unconventional lifestyle." When I was growing up in Birmingham, I was faced with many of the same challenges all Asian teens face in the*

27

U.K.: arranged marriage, dating, cross-racial or cross-caste marriage—caste, for those who don't know, is a deeply entrenched system of social division in India—no talk of sex and sexuality in the home, strict parental control, not fitting in with British culture at large, and so on.

And while many of these are generic teen issues, Asian teens face the added pressure—and tremendous pressure it is, Anjula— of deeply engrained cultural and traditional expectations, as well as strong parental and community influence—

AR: *You mentioned teens, specifically. Why would you say teens are so closely monitored in the Asian community?*

DB: *I believe it's the same all across the board. In other words, not just with Asian teens, but all teens. It's a time of such intensity, all-or-nothing, do-or-die, when the body is budding, and so on.*

AR (laughs): *Hormone poisoning.*

DB: *Yes, to some extent. . . .*

AR: *Then why have a show specifically for Asian families if these are issues all teenagers struggle with?*

DB: *Asian families place enormous value on the concept of family honor, or "izzat." Maintaining a family's good name is a mammoth weight placed squarely on the shoulders of, specifically, teenage girls and women in many Asian families.*

AR: *Yes, it's a concept I know quite well . . . could you talk a bit more on that?*

DB: *Any type of behavior that could potentially tarnish a family's reputation is often strictly punished. Things such as being "immodestly" dressed, fraternizing with the opposite sex, sometimes even laughing too loudly . . . can be interpreted as signs of loose moral character. Therefore, girls, especially, are kept under close watch.*

AR: *Hmm, and given what you just mentioned about hormonal explosions. . . .*

DB: *Exactly. You see the potential for a major clash when, say, Indian parents, born and raised in rural India, raise teens in a place like the U.K., where we've had the sexual revolution, freedom of expression, lingerie adverts and overt sexuality on the telly.*

AR: *Of course. And you, yourself—did you face these same issues with your own parents?*

DB (sad smile): *I was not immune.*

AR: *Tell us about one issue you faced and how you handled it.*

DB: *I'm afraid I didn't really handle it at all. In fact, it quite handled me!*

AR (laughs): *Do tell!*

DB (sighs, but still smiling): *Ah. I was in love with, quite literally, the girl next door. We grew up on the same block in Birmingham. . . .*

(Auntie Kinder! I leaned closer to the monitor.)

. . . we played together as children, our families knew one another, we shared a tender first kiss, snuck off to see each other, the whole bit.

AR: *Sounds absolutely beautiful—I'm waiting for the tragedy to strike. . . .*

DB: *And strike, it did. . . .*

AR: *Oh, dear.*

DB: *Yes. We were "discovered" one evening, er, um. . . .*

(WHAT?? Discovered doing *what*?!?!?!?! I was on the edge of my seat at this point.)

AR: *Being . . . hormonally challenged?*

DB (laughing): *Precisely. Her parents immediately arranged her marriage to a more suitable boy . . . and within weeks, she was married to a respectable, wealthy and influential man of her own caste.*

AR: *How devastating that must've been for you both.*

DB: *Indeed.*

AR: *And that was at what age?*

DB: *Nineteen, we both were.*

AR: *Did you ever try to contact her after that?*

DB (shakes his head): *No, no. It would only complicate matters.*

AR (nodding): *Shortly thereafter, you met your wife, Lalita.*

DB: *Yes, a year after my first love married, I met Lalita and, a year after that, I proposed. She accepted—lucky for me.*

AR: *The story goes that you completed your psychology degree and through friends in the entertainment industry, landed a job on British Radio with a call-in show catering to Britain's Asian-Indian community.*

DB (laughing): *Yes, ironic, innit? All of a sudden, there were aunties, nanis and dadis from all over England, Ireland and Wales, calling me for advice on how to "control" their rebellious teens!*

AR: *But because of the success of that radio show, you were offered your own television show.*

DB (nodding): *Yes.*

AR: *And the rest, as they say. . . .*

DB: *. . . is history.*

AR (gently): *Just as your career was exploding, your wife passed away after a long battle with cancer.*

DB: *Yes, she fought hard, Lalita did.*

AR: *We were all sad to hear the news. She was very devoted to the cause of ending violence against women.*

DB: *Yes, we've set up a fund in her name to benefit organizations serving young women who've been assaulted, sexually, or otherwise, by their boyfriends or partners.*

AR (nodding): A worthwhile cause, indeed.

A pause, then AR, again—switching gears: *Lately you've been making a tentative foray into the dating world again?*

DB (smiling): *So the tabloids report. . . .*

AR: *It's not true, then?*

DB: *I'll leave it at that.*

AR (laughing and turning to the camera): *Well, our time's up with the ever-fascinating Dr. Babaloo, host of his own popular talk show, "Chai with Dr. Babaloo," and author of the recently published* Asian Teens in Britain: A Parent's Handbook. *Check your local listings for the next episode of "Chai," when Dr. Babaloo will be chatting with Salim Khan, the actor most recently coined "Bollywood's answer to Brad Pitt", about the trials and tribulations of raising a Bollywood teen. And don't forget to look on the shelves of your local bookstores for* Asian Teens in Britain.

I'm Anjula Reddy and that's our show for tonight. Please tune in next week when we. . . .

I logged out and stared at the screen for several moments. Wow. Auntie Kinder had pinings for a bona fide TV megastar. Someone she had snuck out to see—and made out with (maybe even *more*??)—before she got married!! Someone who thought Auntie Kinder got married and lived happily ever after with her rich, caste-appropriate Prince Charming.

If only he knew.

Chapter 5

My mom and Mindo Auntie from Canada had been calling each other all week, the way Cindy and I did when there was juicy stuff to share. Whenever I got close to her while she was on the phone, my mom lowered her voice and scurried off to a different room. Could there *possibly* be anything worse than seeing your mom turn into a gossip girl?

Finally, today I found out what the all the secrecy was about. "Jassy, Mindo Auntie has arranged for that young podiatrist-to-be and his mother to come here for a visit. His mother and I have been having some wonderful conversations on the phone—such a lovely family! I will meet his mother in the city while you and the boy chat and get to know one another."

"Couldn't I spend the day smashing my fingers with a mallet, instead?"

"What was that?"

"I said okay."

"Good!" She positively beamed as she searched through her handbag. "Here is a small bit of information for you, just to get you started. The rest you will learn when you meet him, *heh-na?*"

I read the name on the file: *Gurmit Singh Sandhu.* "Gurmit," I said. "Gawd. What is wrong with Indian parents? Why would they name their kid after the most famous amphibian in pre-school?"

Apparently, she didn't think that was as funny as I did. "Jassy, you know it's pronounced Gur-*meeeeeet,*" she said, drawing out the second vowel. She handed me, like, a five-hundred-page file.

"Am I going to be tested on this?"

She took on her stern face. "Jassy, please be serious. This could be your future husband. Won't you at least make an effort?"

I narrowed my eyes. "I thought you said this was supposed to be 'guided dating.' What you're talking about sounds like 'guided marriage.' How can I be serious about that when I haven't even been to my prom? I'm seventeen," I reminded her, yet *again.*

"Precisely why there can be no funny business between the two of you. This is strictly a viewing meeting."

"A *viewing* meeting?"

"Yes, a meeting where the two of you present yourselves to one another to determine if you like what you see."

"*Present* ourselves? Like shopping?"

She squinted her eyes and looked toward the ceiling. "Hmm, I suppose you could see it that way. But I prefer to call it a presentation."

Apparently, some high school juniors went shopping for shoes and skirts with their moms. Me? I was going to be shopping for a life partner in a series of blind dates, as part of the Guided Dating Plan.

She was gazing calmly at me.

I sighed, realizing my options were, um, *none*. "What's he like?" I said finally.

She raised her eyebrows in surprise and clapped her hands together. "I looked through the file, and he seems absolutely perfect, Jassy! I am positive you will simply *adore* him."

"Based on a file?" I wanted to say. But I didn't. Instead, I took the gigantous folder and went to my bedroom to check it out.

I texted Cindy: *hav 2 meet cdn foot doc 2moro*

She called me right back, cackling on the other end. "So, will you guys play footsies? Maybe go for a foot-long sub? Or catch the feet-chur presentation at the movies?"

Honestly, sometimes I wondered why I even liked that girl. "Cut it out, Cin. I'm actually kinda sorta getting into this whole thing a little."

"Seriously? *You?*"

The tone of complete incredulity in her voice bugged me a little. "Yeah. You know—like those cages they showed us in history class, remember? The ones women used to wear under their dresses to make their waists look smaller. I bet they got used to them the way I'll get used to this." I masked the misery in my voice with sarcasm.

She laughed. "It's not that bad, Jazz. You don't *have* to like this guy."

I sighed. "I know. Seriously, though—I'm thinking maybe it won't be that bad. Jeeves's parents had an arranged marriage and they're crazy about each other and my parents have been happily married for twenty years."

"True," she said. "Have you seen a picture of him? Is he at least hot?"

"Not yet . . . but hold on a sec." I turned to the encyclopedia my mother gave me and flipped it open. Sure enough, there was a snapshot taped to the inside of the file folder.

"He's actually not bad," I said, hope swelling in my chest.

"Well . . . maybe he'll be great," she said, not altogether convincingly.

"Hey, if he's on the doctor track at school, he's gotta have *some* brains, right? And if he's not bad looking, I might even have fun. I'm kinda looking forward to it, Cin."

"Then I hope you guys have a *rockin'* time, Jazz. Seriously, what's the worst that can happen?"

"I have to braid the hair on his ears so he can hear me?"

She laughed. "I'm pretty sure hairy ears do not impede hearing."

"True. But hairy backs can impede sexual relations."

"This is true." She giggled. "For your sake, I hope he is totally sexalicious."

"I hope you're right."

Mom and Mindo Auntie had set it up so that I would meet Gurmit after work that Saturday. Every weekend, I went in to Cindy's mom's beauty salon, Redalicious Salon & Spa, to help out—and I got paid to do it. I had been hanging out there since I turned fifteen. It was the one place, next to Auntie Kinder's, that my parents let me go to, because they knew that Cindy was in the "Superstar and Leadership" program (my dad's verbage).

Cindy's older sisters, Mary and Toni, were both having their hair done.

"Toni," Mary said, as Libby the hair-stylist dabbed a dye-soaked paintbrush onto her hair. "Ma says Natural Highlights called and said our payment was late." Mary was taking time off from college to "find herself," and was totally into retro-chic eighties. Today, she was wearing black nail polish, black lipstick, and a red long-sleeved shirt under a fishnet black tank top.

"That's total B.S.," Toni, the older of the two sisters, said, examining one shaved side of her head. "I sent it in way before the deadline. It's a little uneven here," she said, pointing to a spot near the back. The hair stylist went to work evening out Toni's hairline.

I swept the last of the orange curls from the floor into a dust-pan and shook them out into the trash.

Mary shrugged, then turned to me. "You know, Jazz, you would look amazing with a short haircut. You have awesome bone structure."

Oh, no. Wait for it . . . waaaait for it. . . .

"I still don't get why your parents won't let you cut your hair."

Aaaand there it was. "It's against my religion," I said, hoping that answering this same question for the twelve-thousandth time might help it sink in.

Toni sighed. "Oh, Mare, leave it alone, will ya?"

"*Thank* you," I said.

Mary shook her head. "What kind of religion says you can't cut your hair? Honestly. That doesn't make any sense."

"Oh *pull-ease*, Mare," Toni said. "It's the same kind that says women have to be subservient to their husbands in marriage, or women can't be ordained ministers—or the kind that says it's okay for men to have five wives. What the scriptures say and what the men who *read* them say are two different things."

Mary rolled her eyes and turned to me. "Not even a trim? Jeez. You guys aren't even religious, are you?" She waved her fingers around her face. "You would look *so* cute with a shaggy fringe, y'know?"

I sighed, wondering again, for the hundred millionth time, why Ms. Reda had to own a *beauty salon*. Why couldn't she have opened up a restaurant to get over her cheating husband? Or turned to fast food or alcohol, like a decent American?

"No, Mare, not even a trim," I said as Cindy breezed in from behind the curtain separating the waiting room in front from the rest of the salon.

"Funny how your dad is immune to the strict religious doctrine," Toni muttered.

I grunted, but Toni was right. My dad had a beard and turban in some of the old pictures my parents had from India, but ever since they'd been in the U.S., the pictures were of a clean-shaven, short-haired Dad.

Cindy plopped down under an empty hairdryer. "Hey, did Jazz tell you about the tragic *real-life* romance unfolding before our very eyes?"

Mary perked up. "What tragic real-life romance?"

"My Auntie Kinder," I said, un-tensing, now that the focus was off me. "Well, not my real aunt—this woman who used to rent out our basement apartment—she married a total jerk who treated her like crap."

Cindy butted in. "Her parents married her off because they caught her making out with her first *true* love."

"Wait," Toni said, holding up a hand, "they *arranged* her marriage?"

"Yes," I said, moving quickly. I was not in the mood to have the Arranged Marriage Conversation. I hated that one—it put me right smack dab in the middle of the stereotype. I was not doing it today.

"I can't believe they still arrange marriages," Mary said.

Apparently, I was doing it today.

"India has a lower divorce rate than the U.S.," I said, feeling the need to defend a country I'd never been to.

Toni raised one eyebrow. "Really? But are they happy?"

I shrugged. "Is everyone here happy?"

Toni made a face.

"You know," Mary said, "Italians used to have arranged marriages."

Toni nodded. "So did the British. They did it to keep noble lineage within the family."

I leaned on the broom handle. "Maybe that's why Indians do it—to keep everyone from inter-mixing with other castes and religions and races, and stuff."

"Yeah," Toni said, "my mom's traditional Italian family went bonkers when she married our Puerto Rican dad."

"That's why you young people falling in love is so dangerous," Mary said, laughing. Then she narrowed her eyes and said in a sinister whisper, "Because you could fall in love with the *wrong* person!"

"In the old days," Toni added, "if you married someone from lower down on the economic ladder, you could squander your family's fortune."

Cindy grinned. "And now, you could squander your family's culture—or your family's race?"

Toni snorted and was about to say something, but I cut her off. "*Anyway*. Auntie Kinder's parents arranged her marriage to this rich jerk whose parents agreed, but weren't happy about the fact that their new bride was 'too English' and not Indian enough."

I filled them in on the details of Auntie Kinder and Dr. Babaloo's tragic love affair cut short.

"So what did Auntie Kinder do?" Mary whispered, leaning toward me.

I finished sweeping the last of the hair into a dustpan. "From what I've heard through my mom's phone conversations, Auntie Kinder's parents felt bad for putting her in that mess to begin with, so they funded a one-way ticket for her and Pammi to America. They stayed with a cousin for a few months. . . ."

"Then ended up in your basement," Mary said, nodding slowly.

"And *now*. . . ." Cindy's eyes sparkled. "We have located the guy she was caught making out with—her first *true* love. And get this: he's a *star* in England . . . with his own TV show!"

"Get *out*," Mary said, her eyes widening.

"Is he married?" Toni asked.

"He was married at one point," I said, "but his wife passed away a few years ago. And, according to highly credible tabloids sources, he has just started dating again."

"Oh wow," Mary said, hopping down from her chair. "We *have to* get them together again!"

"Right," I said, shaking the hair out into the trash. "I've been wracking my brains trying to figure out how that might happen, but in case you missed it, Mr. True Love, a.k.a. Dr. Babaloo, lives in *England*, and they haven't talked to one another in *years*."

Mary snapped her fingers. "We're talking about love," she said firmly. "Anything is possible."

"Speaking of which," Cindy drawled with a little smile, "Mrs. Dhatt found a soul mate for Jazz – from Canada."

I glared at her.

"Oooooh," Mary said, grinning. "You could cozy up together by the fire after a day on the slopes!"

"Shut up, you guys," I grumbled.

"You don't have to do anything you don't want to, Jazz," Toni said firmly. "Stand your ground. It's important for women to have a choice. No one can make you do anything, girl."

A car pulled up outside and Cindy's boyfriend honked twice.

"Jazz, Wes is here for lunch. Cover me on the cash register?" Cindy said, running to the back room for her jacket.

I sighed, leaned my broom and dustpan in the supply closet and headed to the front desk, daydreaming about what it would be like if that was *me* swooshing out of the door to meet Tyler R., *not* a snow-shoeing podiatrist.

I sat down and clicked on the appointment book: a single-process color, a couple of highlights, some up-do's, waxes, a few sandblasts (basically a full-body dip in wax and every inch de-fuzzed—brows, upper lip, chin, sideburns, arms, full leg, coochie, pits, and toes), and the usual walk-in manicure/pedicures. A typical day at Redalicious Salon & Spa.

The door to the spa was wedged open and Wes, Cindy's boyfriend of two years, waved from his car. "Wha'p'nin', Jazz!" he yelled through the open window of his car.

I smiled and waved back. Wes's family was Jamaican, and every so often he lapsed into Patois (which I'd learned was not actually a Thai noodle dish, but a dialect of English). It was very cool to listen to him—it was like hearing a language that's familiar and unfamiliar at the same time.

Cindy had barely let the door slam behind her when I pulled *Love's Wayward Journey* out of my backpack. For now, I was going to put the real-life tragic romance of Auntie Kinder and Dr. Babaloo—and quite possibly the beginnings of my own tragic fiasco involving Canadian feet—out of my mind and submerge myself into Charlotte's world, a world that was neat and tidy, made more sense, and one that I knew would have a nice, happy ending:

His lips grazed her shoulders as she hung on for life. He growled in desire, watching the flame-haired vixen tremble in his grip. His thoughts were only on the heat emanating from her pores and the scent of strawberries and vanilla in her hair.

He wondered when he had begun to love her, this exasperating, stubborn feline creature from the big city. She fought him on everything. He pressed her hard against the brick wall and she moaned quietly. A small smile curved his lips as he watched her heavy lidded eyes. Yes, she fought him on everything. Everything except this.

He slipped his hand under the layers of her skirt, shuddering when his fingers discovered warm bare skin. . . .

"AHEM!"

My head jerked up at the same time that I snapped my book shut, sending it flying across the room in the process.

Standing in front of me, with an amused expression on his face, was Jeevan "Jeeves-to-my-peeps" Sahota.

Jeeves lived at the other end of my street. In first grade, he walked into the FSL class, skinny and snotty, with one of those prehistoric metal lunchboxes in one hand. He kept wiping the back of his hand across his dribbling nose and shifting his weight from one foot to the other like he had to pee while the teacher introduced him to the class.

In grade school, because there were so few of us brown kids in the school, we avoided one another like bad breath. Already, as it was, we in the FSL class got plenty of unnecessary, unwanted attention. If we weren't getting the contents of our lunches buried in the sandbox, we were busy ensuring the leg bands of our underwear stayed securely around our legs and not shoved up into wedgies.

Until high school, of course. There we met kids from some of the surrounding neighborhoods. Then, all of a sudden, we were surrounded by varying shades of brown and tan. Our high school looked a lot more like my mom's spice rack, with more cinnamon, nutmeg, and garam masala sprinkled in with the usual salt and pepper.

In high school, I witnessed the awesome influx of bindi-bos, turbanators (hunky turbaned jocks), and broners (brown stoners). That was when Arvind "Call me Rob" Kumar finally started using his own name again, aspiring bindi-bos that I grew up with finally found their voices and claimed their inalienable right to jiggle alongside their blonde counterparts, and brown-on-brown hook-ups reached record highs.

But I meet Jeeves before any of that happened. Before our mothers started having regular chai chats and forcing us into playdates for years to come. And before Jeeves himself, got a blast of allergy shots and became Mr. Six-Foot-Four-Star-Basketball-Forward at Maple Ridge. Gone was the gangly, peachfuzzy, honking supra-geek; in his place was a flying, rotating-in-the-air basketball machine with an IQ in the six-figure range, and a throng of hoochies in every shade and hue following him between classes.

And still, the image firmly etched into my brain was the one from that first day of school. But it was Superdude Jeeves that stood on the other side of the front desk now.

"Oh, hey! Jeeves! How are ya!" I said, all mega-cheerful, as I shot out of my seat to snatch my book off the floor.

"Whatcha reading?" he asked, peering over the counter.

I stretched a huge smile across my face. "Nothing!" I could feel the beads of sweat forming under my nose.

He grinned. "Doesn't *look* like nothing."

I dropped my smile and changed my tactic. "What are you doing here?" I asked, raising my eyebrows. "Manicure? Wax? No, let me guess . . . highlights!"

"Ha ha," he said, shifting his weight from one foot to the other.

Toni once said that guys are super predictable. If you wanted to go on the offense, question their masculinity.

"My mom. It's her birthday. Not today. Next week. My dad. He said to get her a gift. Certificate."

"Riiiight. Your *mom*," I said, stuffing my novel under a stack of promo flyers.

"Ha. *Ha*. You're a riot."

I pulled out the book of red-and-gold gift certificates, tore one off the top, and wrote out the number and date. I looked up. "How much?"

He shifted his weight again. "I don't know . . . What do people usually get?"

I smiled. He was so uncomfortable, it was kind of cute. I picked up one of the service brochures and pointed out a few options.

"You could get her a 'Crimson Care' package – massage, facial, manicure, pedicure . . . or how about the 'Scarlet Sinsational'? It's got everything the Crimson package has, *plus* a seaweed wrap and paraffin manicure. Oh, I almost forgot about the 'Ruby Retreat'—same as the Scarlet package, but with hot and cold stone massage, exfoliating body rub, and an aromatherapy consult."

When I looked back at him, his eyes were glazed over. "Helloooo?" I said, "Am I speaking Konkani?"

(My dad's verbage. Dad: *Why don't you join the chess/debate/other geekarrific team?*

Me: *Huh?*

Dad: *What, am I speaking Konkani?)*

Jeeves shook his head. "Why would anyone pay to be wrapped in seaweed?"

"For smooth, supple, pliant, radiant skin," I quoted from the brochure. "Why don't you get the 'Crimson Care'? That way, your mom can upgrade if she wants when she comes in."

"Deal," he said, slapping down a wad of bills.

I rang up his purchase, counted out his change, and held out the envelope. "Here you go. Thank you for choosing Redalicious Salon."

He grinned, relieved. "Thanks," he said, shoving the envelope into his jacket pocket.

I waited for him to turn around and walk back out the door, but he stood cemented to the spot with his hands shoved deep in his pockets.

"Was there something else?" I asked.

"Oh, uh. No. I just. . . ." He cleared his throat and started walking backward to the door. "I'll just, ah, I mean . . . okay, bye." He slammed into the door, turned around, opened it and took off.

I watched him dart around the corner and shook my head. Pretty clumsy for a guy who was real suave-bola with the bindibos and hoochies at school. I guess it just goes to show that you can reinvent yourself all you want, but get around the people who knew you when? Super Dude to Ultra Geek in three point five seconds.

I pulled *Love's Wayward Journey* out from underneath the promo flyers. I read as much of the five hundred page epic as I could before my mom came to transport me to my big date with could-be-future-husband, Gurmit.

Chapter 6

My mom picked me up after work and drove me to the coffee shop where she and "the boy's mother" agreed we should first set eyes on our future spouse. Then my mother drove off to meet his mother for lunch.

I opened the door and took a quick glance around. He was pretty easy to spot. There was an encyclopedia file—that looked a lot like the one my mom had given me—on the table in front of him, and he was sipping a Caramel Smackuccino in one of the overstuffed armchairs. I looked closely at his profile, taking a peek at the photo I'd unstuck from the front cover of his file, as he sat with his nose in a thick, hardcover book.

I walked over to him. "Um. You can't be Gurmit?"

He jerked his head out of the book he'd been reading. "Oh—!"

"Sorry, I didn't mean to scare you."

He stood up and shook my hand. He was wearing a crisp, tan, button-up shirt and dark jeans.

I wondered if his mother made him go upstairs and change at least three times like mine had: *Jassy, first impressions are important! This is a future doctor and he is in Mindo's extended family—you cannot meet him looking like a beggar.*

"No, I . . . hi, you're obviously Jasbir."

"Jazz."

He smiled, showing a row of perfectly straight, white, dental-brochure teeth. "Right. I'm Mit."

I grinned. "Nice to meet you, Mit."

I plopped down in the chair across from him and he sat back down in his. We sat like that for what felt like ages, saying nothing. I looked around at the few tables where people sat, some with laptops, others with books. A couple of moms with squirming babies on their laps. An old man sleeping with his head thrown back, hands folded on his belly, mouth open.

I tried to keep my eyes from sliding back to Gurmit. But can I just say (from the little bit I did catch of him when he wasn't looking)—Gurmit Singh Sandhu was kinda sexy (!). Who knew?

He had the longest eyelashes I'd ever seen on a guy, no hair on his knuckles and ears (therefore, presumably, none on his back, either), and he had that kind of pretty, boy-band-singer kind of face. The kind that mothers love.

We began speaking at the same time.

"Look, I don't—"

"I just want to—"

Then we both said, "You first."

He laughed and held up his hand. "Okay, me first."

Excuse me? What happened to ladies first? Shouldn't he be *trying* to be a gentleman? Didn't his mother have that "first impression" talk with him?

He smiled.

SIGH. "Okay, go ahead."

"I just want to be clear that I'm not in the least bit interested in getting married."

I exhaled loudly. "Me, neither!"

He widened his eyes. "Awesome! I was so worried you'd be one of those girls I'd have to scrape off, you know?"

"No," I said, slowly. "But I'm glad you don't want to get married, either. I was afraid you'd be an uptight, nerdy mama's boy."

He shuddered. "Trust me, I know exactly what you mean. My mom's been on my case to date lately."

"Really? Why? Just use the college excuse."

His eyes flicked away. "She's concerned that I'm not 'showing interest.' She finally decided she'd give me some help and *forced* some girls on me."

"I'm sure she didn't have to force them," I said shyly. Then I quickly added, "I mean, it's not as if you're repulsive or anything."

He smiled, reaching out and tapping my upper arm. "Thanks. You're not bad, either."

Not bad. Ugh. I waited for that thrill you get when a hot guy touches you. Nothing. I slumped a little in my seat. Maybe it would come later?

I looked back at him hopefully, and saw that he'd been staring at me.

I felt like I'd just been caught stealing, or cheating on a math test, or something.

"What are you thinking about?" he asked, almost like he was mad.

"Huh? Um . . . I, uh. . . ."

"Listen, Jazz," he said, pressing his lips together for a moment before continuing. He looked around, then leaned in. "There's a reason I haven't been showing interest in girls," he whispered. He cupped a hand to the side of his mouth. "I'm gay."

I stared at him for a moment. "Wait," I said, shaking my head and grinning. "I thought you just said. . . ."

"I did."

I swallowed hard. "But."

He looked at me quietly and waited.

I shook my head again. "You're Indian!"

He gasped in exaggerated awe. "You *are* in the genius program at your school!"

"And you're *hot*." I couldn't help myself.

He crossed his arms in front of his chest and gave me an irritated look.

I stared at him. "Are you serious? 'Cuz you don't have to—I'm not so crazy about this whole set up either—"

He held a hand up to stop me. "No, I *wanted* to meet you."

"Wow," I said slowly. "What a waste."

"Augh!" he said, throwing his arms up. "I *hate* when people say that. I bet there are a ton of lesbos out there who say the same thing about you: what a waste she's straight."

"You did not just say that," I said as his words seeped in. "If our mothers could only hear this conversation."

We both looked at one another, then cracked up at the same time.

"I don't think I've ever met a gay Indian before," I said finally. "Never mind a gay, Indian, Punjabi, Sikh. At least not that I've known of."

He shrugged. "Yeah, they took that clause out of the Gay Rules—the one that made it mandatory to introduce yourself as Gay Gurmit, or Dykey Davinder."

That cracked us up again. I wished I had a voice recorder so that I could use this conversation at my pleasure against my mom some day.

"Do your parents know?" I asked.

His laughter petered off. "No."

"Oh." Wow. And I thought keeping my scandalous romance novels a secret was hard.

He twirled a plastic straw around his fingers. "My dad once shouted 'There are no gay people in India!' during a documentary that I 'accidentally' ordered from Netflix when I was hoping I could come out to them."

We were both quiet for a moment. I knew what it was like to have love restricted and dictated—that was my life. I so, so, OMG, *so* badly wanted to be able to date like Cindy and walk around with my finger hooked through the belt loop of a guy's jeans while he gazed into my eyes . . . and to be able to do it in *public,* without being terrified of getting caught and facing who-knew-what. But to have your type of love *hated*, or not even acknowledged as being for real . . . that was a whole other thing.

I couldn't think of a thing to say, so instead I did what he had done earlier. I lightly thumped his upper arm.

He looked up at me with a small smile and took a sip from his Smackuccino as I thumbed through his file.

"Jazz . . . when I found out you were in the genius program, I thought you might be cooler—you know, more 'aware' than the other girls my mom kept throwing at me. That's why I wanted to meet you. I was hoping we could make a . . . a deal."

I raised an eyebrow. "What kind of deal?"

He looked down before continuing. "My parents are really on my back about marriage and stuff lately—I think mostly because they suspect what's up."

"Yeah, most Indian parents don't want their sons even *thinking* about marriage, or the opposite sex, until they're done with school."

"Well . . . not mine. I'm getting the third degree because I'm *not* thinking about the opposite sex."

I heaved a sigh. "We just can't win."

"I was hoping we could, you know . . . maybe play along for a little while. Act like this is going well and that we're into the whole thing." He looked like a hopeful little kid on Santa's knee. "You know, so that our parents will leave us alone."

"You mean be all 'Let's get married,' and stuff?"

He nodded, not taking his eyes off my face.

I thought about his proposal. It might not be a bad thing, actually. It could mean that 1) my mom would stop spreading snapshots on the coffee table every weekend and leave me alone; 2) I'd be expected to spend more time with Mit, who I was enjoying hanging out with; and 3) It would buy me some time—time that could be spent searching on my own for my true love (which I'd now decided was definitely Tyler R., because the fates seemed to be throwing me at him. Plus, he was hot, sexy, possibly rich, and at least brown—if not "Indian enough" for my parents).

"Okay," I said, nodding slowly. "But what if they start taking things really seriously? Like, what if they start . . . y'know, making preparations or something?"

"I don't think mine'll do that. I'm only *eighteen*. I mean they're not insane—not completely, anyway. Do you think yours will start on actual preparations?"

"No," I snapped, far too quickly. I am a Scorpio and, if nothing else, it means I am fiercely loyal. As much as I can't stand my parents sometimes, I will not admit my parents are more insanely dictatorial than someone else's. "I'm just saying, what *if.*"

"It'll be fine, Jazz. Watch. They'll be happy we've both found someone suitable to focus our attention on, instead of looking around at all kinds of *unsuitable* people, and they've fulfilled their responsibility as our parents in finding us a good match and possible life partner. We'll be stress free for the next couple of years. Then you'll do something unforgivable and we'll break up." He sat back looking quite pleased with himself.

"*I* do something unforgivable?"

He waved away my question. "We can figure out the details later. What do you think?"

"I will *not* be the one doing the unforgivables, dude. I've got enough crap to deal with from my mom as it is. The last thing I need is to shatter her hopes and dreams for my marriage to the perfect, suitable, gay Punjabi boy."

"Fine. We'll cross that bridge when we get to it. Deal?" He held out his hand.

I shook it.

We hung out a bit more, chatting about the boys we were crushing on and the best shades of nail polish for brown skin until our mothers came to pick us up. When we were introduced to each other's mothers, you should've seen the grins. Our mothers were beaming so hard—they could've guided ships through pea-soup fog with all those gleaming teeth.

We both went home and told our mothers how great a time we had and that we really liked each other. It made for a totally stress-free weekend with my mom in the best mood since, like, *ever*.

And then, on Monday, Tyler R. blew my entire world apart.

Chapter 7

OH. MY. GAAAAWWWWD. Tyler R touched me. He TOUCHED me!!!! I was on my way out the door, to meet Cindy and her sisters for lunch at Tony's Diner, when I realized I'd forgotten my wallet in my jacket pocket. I told Cindy I'd catch up with them and ran to my locker to grab aforementioned wallet.

Out of nowhere, I felt these warm fingers on my elbow. TYLER R.'s fingers. (Shudder). I totally died. Right there.

"Hi, I'm Tyler."

No *kidding.* He was *this* close to my face. I knew it was my turn to say something, but for the life of me couldn't remember what on earth it could possibly be.

"And you aaaare. . . ."

"Ahhh. . . ."

He leaned over my shoulder, brushing the back of it with his chest, and read the cover of my composition notebook. "Jazz Dhatt."

Oh, why, oh *why* couldn't I have had a cooler name? Dear God, *please* give my knees strength to hold me up.

Tyler grinned. "There's so much you can do with that name."

I stopped myself from shouting, *It's yours! Do whatever you want with it!* I managed, instead, to squeak out, "It's all been done—" (giggle) "—Jazz dat thing, all dat jazz, jazz dis and jazz dat. . . ."

Nice, Jazz. So, SO lame.

His lip curled up on one side, ending in a perfectly lickable little dimple. "Nice to meet you, Jazz," he said, walking backward. "See you around."

I stood there nodding vigorously, looking like I should have a balloon above my head with the words, "Uh-huh, uh-huh, uh-huh." No doubt there was a line of drool making a lazy descent to the floor, while he walked to the end of the hall and rounded the corner.

Then, in a befuddled daze, I walked to Tony's diner to meet Cindy, Mary, and Toni.

They had already ordered when I got there. "Girl, what took you so long?" Cindy asked, dipping a giant, greasy french fry into a vat of gravy. "Mare, pass me that salt?"

"What's with you?" Toni said, raising an eyebrow ring. "You look like you just saw, oh, I don't know . . . Einstein or something. Isn't that who you brainiacs worship?"

"You ordering, Jazz?" Mary asked, picking tomatoes out of her sandwich.

"Tyler R. *touched* me."

They all paused for a beat. Then at the same time:

"Who's Tyler R.?"

"Touched you *how*?"

"No WAY!!"

Cindy snapped her fingers. "Details. *Now*."

I shook my head slowly. "He just came up behind me and introduced me. I mean himself. And his chest rubbed up against my shoulder. Right here," I said, turning around and pointing to where Tyler R.'s CHEST had recently been.

"Who's Tyler R.?" Mary asked again.

Cindy closed her jaw enough to answer quickly. "Only the hottest, hottest, *hottest* hottie at Maple Ridge! Omigosh, *Jazz*."

"I know!" I squealed. "Can you believe it? I can't. I can not believe it. Why would Tyler R. want to talk to *me*? He has his pick of the entire school. Every butt-crack-baring, *Juicy*-bottomed, cantaloupe-boobed. . . ."

"Don't forget ditzy. . . ." said Cindy.

". . . hair-tossing hoochie he could ever want," I finished.

Toni sighed loudly. "I hate when members of my gender do this. Not only did you two unfairly and unjustly put down all of these women, but *you*," she pointed a fork at me, "you completely devalued yourself and your best qualities."

Cindy looked at Toni for a second. "Okay, I hate to admit it, but maybe she has a point, Jazz. Maybe Tyler's deeper than that, you know? Maybe he's tired of the ditzes—" she glanced at Toni, "or girls *pretending* to be ditzes—and wants someone who's not afraid to be smart. You know—someone who can string a sentence together and be proud of it."

Toni grumbled and was about to say something, but Mary interrupted. "No guy wants conversation," she said authoritatively. "They want Pamela Anderson up top, Beyoncé in back, and Jessica Simpson in the head."

"*Exactly*," I said, dropping my shoulders. "I am not even *close* to any of that."

"Well, whatever it is," Cindy said, grinning, "he rubbed up on you."

I rolled my eyes. "He did not 'rub up' on me."

Still, even if he didn't, B-52 bombers buzzed around in my belly every time I thought of that moment of contact.

After lunch, Toni and Mary took off to meet their boyfriends before going back to the salon, and Cindy and I walked back to school.

"What's up?" Cindy asked.

"Huh?" We were walking up the stone path to the back entrance of the school, near the bio labs, where the fragrance of formaldehyde greeted us on impact.

"You're pouting."

"I am not."

She gave me a look.

I shrugged. "I just wish people would see me as more than just brainy sometimes, you know?"

She grabbed my shoulder and gently shook it. "You're smart, Jazz! That's a *good* thing, remember?"

Sure, easy for her to say. She already had a boyfriend who worshipped her.

"Okay, this is me," she said as we neared the hall where her locker was. "Look, don't sweat it. Obviously, Tyler R. likes what he sees—and he'll like you even more when he gets to know you." She flashed me a smile and bounced down the hall.

I dragged my feet toward my locker.

Obviously, Tyler R. likes what he sees.

Yeah, maybe. Or maybe he needs help writing an essay.

"Every Sunday my mom and dad inflict a Bollywood movie on me. They have this idea that watching cheesy Hindi films, and even cheesier Punjabi films, will balance out all the American images I get on a daily basis; that I'll somehow absorb my Indian heritage through song and dance and stay connected to my roots."

Jeeves laughed. "We have regular cheese-fests, too, except I think my parents do it more for themselves than for me—it keeps *them* connected to their roots."

We were walking home after school like we usually did when Jeeves didn't have basketball practice. Cindy, Jeeves, and I lived within blocks of one another, and had been walking to and from school together since we were all kids. Today Cindy was hanging out with Wes, so it was just me and Jeeves.

I stopped to adjust the weight of my backpack. "Huh. I never thought of it that way."

We walked in a kind of thoughtful silence for a few minutes.

"You know, I don't really mind them, actually," I admitted. "Some of them, I really like—but they're not the ones my parents want to watch—like I really liked *Jadu* and *3 Idiots*. But my parents want to watch the old ones—if they're in black and white, even better."

Jeeves smirked. "I know. My dad's seen *Mother India*, like, twelve times."

"I guess, in a way, those movies do keep me connected," I said. "I'm reminded of how differently my parents see things sometimes, you know?"

He nodded. "Like the fact that it's still revolutionary to show two people kissing on the lips."

"*Totally.* I mean, compare that to, like, *anything* on cable."

"No wonder they get all freaked out."

I looked at him. "Somehow I get the feeling that my parents are probably just a *tad* more freaked out than yours."

He shrugged. "You're a girl."

"What's that supposed to mean?"

"It's just the way it is." Then he turned and smiled. "You could get pregnant and destroy your entire family's reputation, including all the ancestors and future generations."

"So?" I said, bristling. "You could get a girl pregnant and get your butt beat by her entire family."

He laughed and reached for a rock. "That ain't happening."

"What if it did?"

"It won't. Your parents are big on Education, mine are big on Responsibility. I think instead of slapping my butt, my parents had the obstetrician tattoo the word 'Responsibility' into my brain after I was born." He let the rock sail across the street and looked at me. "What if it happened to you?"

"You must be suffering from delusional insanity."

"Is that a technical term?" He said, laughing again and putting his arm around me. I think this shocked him as much as it did me, because he promptly removed his arm and shoved his hands deep into his pockets.

He cleared his throat. "Hey, you wanna come over tonight and go through Mr. Stone's Latin assignment?"

I thought about Stone's latest assignment—to write an entire story in Latin, using only the words we'd learned so far—and groaned. "You mean the one that's due next week?"

He nodded. "Yup." After a moment, he added, "Maybe afterward we could watch one of my mom's DVDs. It would be like a study: The Effects of Cheesy Bollywood Films on FSL juniors."

I laughed. "My mom would be *tha-rilled* that I would actually initiate watching a Hindi film, especially if it's educational."

"One of the ones my mom's been hounding me and my dad to watch is *Dilwale Dulhaniya Leh Jayenge*."

"I think I had to take antibiotics for that once."

He grinned. "Apparently, it won major awards and was one of the biggest box-office successes in Indian history. But it's not educational—it's a cheesy love story."

"That sounds right up my alley. But as you so kindly pointed out, I'm a *girl* with Indian parents who are freaked out by lascivious American media and paranoid of anything their daughter does outside of school."

"Our parents have known each other for years, Jazz. I know Auntie will be fine with you coming over to do Latin homework."

He was right. my parents were friends with everyone, regardless of nationality, race, class, caste, whatever. But when it came to their daughter's choice in life partner, *that's* when everything hit the fan.

I rolled my eyes. "Years, schmears. My parents turn into the FBI Counter-terrorism Squad when I'm talking to a male *cousin*, Jeeves. But Latin homework—now *that* could work."

"Course it will." He grinned. "As Uncle says, I'm in the 'Superstar and Leadership' program, too. C'mon, hang out with regular folk for a night."

I thwacked him on the shoulder. "*You* are not regular folk, dude."

And actually, getting my parents to agree to doing Latin homework at Jeeves's place was a not as hard as I'd thought. Could be that my mom was so over the moon with me liking Mit, that in her eyes, other boys were no longer a threat.

My parents still shot zinging glances at one another over my head and grilled me about how long Mrs. Sahota would be there, and where she'd be in the house (yes, *really*). And I did whine and moan a lot about how important Latin is for any career related to medicine or the sciences—and how bad I was at it and how Jeeves was a total whiz. But in the end they seemed comfortable enough with the whole thing to let me go.

So, I had dinner with my mom after my dad left for work, then grabbed my books and headed over to Jeeves's house.

His mother answered the door. "Jazz! Come in, *beta*."

Jeeves's parents were big city dwellers in India, not rural villagers like mine. So they had a British lilt to their English and they were way more caught up on modern-day mass culture than my parents.

Mrs. Sahota took my umbrella and shook it out on their porch. "Jeevan's downstairs, dear."

"Thanks, Auntie," I said, bounding down the stairs.

Jeeves looked up from jotting something down in his notebook. "Hey. This is *not* easy."

As we plodded through the Latin assignment together, I thanked the universe, the stars, and the Milky Way that I wasn't dumb enough to have tried it on my own. Jeeves really was good at Latin—especially verb conjugation, and I was good at putting the words into sentences that made sense. We made a pretty good team.

At one point, Mrs. Sahota came down and set a couple of glasses of juice on the table for us, then went back upstairs.

When we were done, Jeeves got up and stretched. "I could go for some mindless entertainment now," he said, grabbing the remote. He went and sat on the edge of the sofa.

I finished my final sentence, packed up my books, then went to check out their DVD collection. "Wow, your mom has, like, every HBO series ever made."

"Yeah, some of those are my dad's, too."

I browsed the titles on another shelf. "And a *huge* Bollywood collection. My parents always rent them."

"That is all my mom's. She wants to be able to go back to certain scenes and watch them over and over again."

I stared at him. "Wow—she's really into them, huh?"

He looked at me for a moment. "I guess it's a lot like . . . oh, I don't know—romance novels, maybe?"

I snapped my mouth shut. "It is *not* the same." But when I thought about it, I knew he was right.

"Come on, Jazz." He was trying not to smile. "They're all about some girl resisting her obvious soul mate, then finally realizing he was right underneath her nose all along." He put the back of his hand to his forehead and mock swooned. "Or how about this one—girl meets bad boy, whom she hates in the beginning, then realizes she's madly in love with him by the end of the book."

"You talk like you know," I said. Then I narrowed my eyes at him. "And they are not *all* like that."

He burst out laughing. "Yeah, and neither are these movies, right? Pop that one in and if it's not what I just said, I'll do your Latin homework for the next two weeks."

I looked at the DVD he was pointing at. "How do I know you haven't already seen it?"

He gave me a *you-can't-be-serious* look.

When I didn't budge, he walked to the bottom of the stairs and called up. "Hey, Mom—Jazz wants to know if I've already seen DDLJ!"

After a short pause, we both heard, quite clearly, Mrs. Sahota's uproarious laughter.

He turned back to me. "Satisfied?"

"What happens if I win?"

"You won't," he said. "But if you do, you have to come over for the next two weekends to do your homework."

"That's it?"

He shrugged. "I'm confident."

I thought for a moment. It *would* be nice not to have to worry about my Latin homework for a couple of weeks. And, given the seriously cornball plotlines of the old movies my parents watched, there was no way this movie could be anything like *Love's Wayward Journey*, or even *Dhoom*—one of my favorite Bollywood movies of all time.

"Okay," I said finally. "Bring on the cheese."

He popped in the DVD.

"Sheesh, how corny is that?" I said, guffawing for the sixty-third time in the first ten minutes.

He gave me bored look. "Just chill for a minute, Dhatt. Wait."

"Are you sure you haven't seen this before? Cuz you seem to know what's coming up. . . ."

"They're all the same, Jazz—that's my point."

He was so smug, I had the urge to blow a raspberry at him. I shoved myself back into the sofa and stewed quietly for a while, even though I felt myself getting sucked into the movie.

When there was a part that I just had to comment on, I leaned across for the remote and hit *Pause*. "Did he just tell her to shut up? And did she just *apologize* to him after he told her to shut up?"

Jeeves sighed. "He's messing with her. It's all good-natured."

"Right. Good-natured abuse. Of course." I hit Play again.

But after all of the "good-natured messing around," things got WAY better. I was so into it that I didn't say another word until the end of the movie.

Jeeves's mom popped in every time a song came on and stayed until it was over. Then she bounced on up the stairs, humming the song she'd just heard.

"Wow," I said, nodding and turning to Jeeves, "it was actually better than I thought. Still had some stinky fermented dairy parts, but not bad at all. Let's check out the Special Features."

"But it's so corny," he said, mimicking me. He was grinning from ear to ear.

"Shut up," I said, grabbing for the remote.

He gasped, put a hand to his chest and leaned back. "Did you just tell me to *shut up*?"

I laughed. "Okay, smart butt, you made your point. Now put on the freaking Special Features!"

"We have a deal, Dhatt."

"Yeah, yeah. I'm here for the next two weekends for homework."

He actually blushed. "You know, you don't have to. I was just trying to make a point."

"Well, you made it."

For a brief moment, there was an awkward silence. I fiddled with the fringe on one of the throw cushions.

Jeeves cleared his throat. "I did, you know."

I looked up from my fiddling. "You did what?"

He raised his arms in victory. "I *won*!" He cupped his hands around his mouth and made the sound of cheering crowds. "And the defending champion once again comes out on top, ladies and gentlemen!"

I punched the Play button to turn on the Special Features so I could drown out Jeeves's cheering for himself, and found myself steadily falling in huge, star-worshipping infatuation with a young Shah Rukh Khan. He wasn't too far from my current novel-crush, Enrique, in the way he pursued the love of his life across a continent, to save her from an unwanted arranged marriage. *SIGH*.

"I can see why it did so well," Jeeves said, finally getting serious and powering off the DVD player.

"Mmhmm. Me, too."

"Six *years* in the theaters—can you think of any movies here that played for six straight years?"

I shook my head while making a mental note to find out more about Shah Rukh Khan on the Internet. I'd seen other movies with him where he was older, but had no idea he was kind of a hottie when he was younger.

We chatted a bit with his mom about school and colleges we were considering, and then I got ready to leave. Jeeves walked me out onto the porch.

"Are your parents going to pick a girl for you, Jeeves?" I said, thinking about my recent "date" with Mit.

"Crap, I hope not—you've seen my mom's taste in movies. She might find someone who sings and runs behind trees when I lean in for a kiss."

I laughed. "How do you know you won't like some coy singing? Those thongster bindi-bos spoiling you?"

I *so* wished I hadn't said that.

For a minute, he turned so red I almost thought he was choking on something.

After what had to be the most awkward silence in history, he finally shrugged. "They probably won't pick someone for me."

"Really?" I almost collapsed with relief; that silence was more than I could bear. "Even though that's what *they* did and it seems to have worked?"

"I guess they figure it's a crap-shoot. Whether you pick your own, or whether they pick for you, you never know if it's going to work out. We know some families who are totally happy and their parents had arranged marriages, and then we know some who are miserable. Same with families where the parents picked their own partners." He grinned. "The ones who had 'love marriages.'" He used his Punjabi accent for that phrase.

I smiled. "Wow. I wonder if your parents would consider adopting a brilliant and talented seventeen-year-old. They are *so* cool."

"They already have a brilliant and talented seventeen-year-old."

"Oh, true—I meant to say, a brilliant, talented, and stunningly attractive seventeen-year-old . . . *that* they do not have."

He laughed, then looked thoughtfully out into the street. "You know, I think there are valid points either way—pro-arranged marriage and against."

"Easy for you to say. You don't have parents who put hidden cameras in every room of the house."

"Your parents don't have hidden cameras, Jazz."

"I wouldn't put it past them. I could even see them installing one in my locker."

"It's not that bad, Dhatt. Besides, I got problems, too, you know."

"Oh, please, Sahota. What could you possibly have to worry about? Your parents think the sun rises and sets with you. No— they think you *are* the sun."

He drew in a deep breath and stretched his arms out. "Yep, a lot of people think that."

"Ha, ha."

"No, seriously. Your parents just want to make sure you're okay. And mine, too. Obviously, they'd prefer I end up with someone clean and decent—with most of her teeth intact."

"What if she was clean and decent, with about three yellow, but good, teeth?"

He snorted. "That's a tough one."

Another awkward silence. We seemed to be racking those up tonight.

"Well," I said. "I guess I should go."

"Yeah."

"I'll see you at school?"

He nodded. "Where else?"

"Okay, so, bye. Um, thanks for the cheese."

"No probs. Anytime. See ya, Jazz."

As I walked the half block to my house, I wondered how I'd never noticed that Jeeves looked a little like the young Shah Rukh Khan in DDLJ.

Chapter 8

"*English with Mr. Hall* is quite possibly the biggest waste of time in history," Cindy said, pulling the rubber band out of her hair. "Jaaaaazz, knock, knock!" She actually tried to knock on my head.

I moved away just in time. "Sorry. I'm thinkin'."

"Don't hurt yourself," Jeeves said with a smirk.

I gave him a bright fake-smile.

"What's up?" Cindy asked. "You've been quiet the whole walk home."

"I was thinking about that blind date my mom set me up on."

They both stopped short.

"How'd it *go*?" Cindy shrieked.

Jeeves stared at me. "*What* blind date?"

"Sorry, I forgot to mention it in the midst of our Bollywood cheesefest. His name is Gurmit Singh Sandhu."

Cindy made a *yikes!* face. "Doesn't sound promising."

"And he's gay," I said with a flourish.

Jeeves's mouth dropped open. "*Gay*, gay? How could you forget *that*? He's Indian?"

Cindy squealed and slapped a hand against the binder she held in the crook of her arm. "I LOVE it!"

"Dude. With a name like Gurmit Singh, he'd better be Indian. And *Punjabi*."

He shook his head. "Get the f—"

Cindy grabbed my arm. "Omigosh, Jazz. You are *so* in the clear! You guys can be like girlfriends and hang out forever and your parents will be thrilled!"

"That's what he said!"

"It's *perfect*," she said, giving my arm a squeeze.

Jeeves was still shaking his head. "Gay?"

Cindy glanced at him. "Deal with it, dude."

"I am, it's just . . . wow."

"I know, right?"

"As if it isn't hard enough being us," he said.

I jabbed my finger in the air. "Totally! Like, dating is the total forbidden land, for *straight* brown kids."

"Um, unless it's 'guided' dating," Cindy interjected with a grin.

I gave her a sour look.

Jeeves kicked a stone in his path. "But if it's *not* guided—or strictly controlled by your parents, and you get caught, there can be serious consequences, depending on your parents and who you get caught *with*."

"Like if they're the wrong caste or something?" Cindy asked.

He nodded, blowing hair out of his eyes.

"Speaking of which," I said, "Auntie Kinder."

Cindy's eyes lit up. "You have a plan?"

I shook my head. "Not yet."

"What about Auntie Kinder?" Jeeves asked.

Cindy and I filled him in, but before we could say her long-lost-love's name—.

"Dr. Babaloo!" he said, dropping his jaw.

My eyes rounded. "You've heard of him?"

"My mom orders all his DVDs online. Her faves are *The Parent-Teen Trap* and *How to Keep Your Marriage Zinging*." He shuddered.

"No WAY!" I could feel the synapses firing in my brain. "I've been searching all over the Net for contact information for him, but on his site, they only list the studios they tape at! There is a Contact page, and every time I try to use it I get an error message."

"You'd think somebody would let him know the site's not working," Cindy said, making a face.

"He's old," Jeeves said. "Maybe he's not good with the internet. I'll check the DVDs."

"If he's such a big shot, he should have people doing that for him. I bet Dr. Phil has somebody doing his website." Cindy said. She cocked her head and looked at me. "What're you planning to say to him?"

"I have no idea."

We arrived at Cindy's street and she gave me and Jeeves a quick hug each. "I'm sure you'll come up with something. . . . It just keeps getting better and better! First Tyler R., then your gay fiancé, and now all this romance and intrigue . . . and *fame*. Even if it's not Dr. Phil fame." She flashed her perfectly even, perfectly white teeth and waved as she bounced up the street to her house.

"What's she talking about?" The look on Jeeves's face was jarring. Major intensity.

"Huh?"

He looked away, then said casually to the sidewalk, "She said something about Tyler R. What's she talking about?"

"Nothing. You know Cindy," I said with a laugh that didn't even convince *me*. "She has an uber-active imagination."

We walked in silence for the half-block to his house.

He stopped at the end of his driveway and shoved his hands deep into his pockets. "Tyler R.," he said, looking up at the sky. "What do girls see in him?"

Um, other than the fact that he's hot, popular, athletic, and quite possibly rich? I shrugged. "He seems like a nice guy."

He made a yeah-right face. "Every hot honors and FSL girl is hanging off him. Is it the whole good-girl/bad-boy thing?"

I raised my eyebrows. "What're you talking about?"

He shook the hair out of his eyes, then looked at me. "Just take it easy, Jazz. You and Tyler R. . . . you're not in the same league."

Just what was *that* supposed to mean? But before I could ask, he said, "See ya," turned on his heel, and walked into his house.

My face burned as I walked past the five houses between his and mine. You've got some nerve, Mr. Geekoid-Turned-Hyper-Hunk! You wanna talk about not being in Tyler R.'s league? Let's talk about snot and zits and constant wedgies! Huh? How about *that*?

And just when I was thinking how nice it was to have him around! To not have to explain why I can't cut my hair, and why it is a HUGE deal to be Gay While Indian and another HUGE deal that Auntie Kinder might've had a significant relationship before marriage!

When I got home, I said hi to my unconscious father on the couch and marched straight upstairs to my room. I was about to sit down and compose a hate email to Jeeves, letting him know exactly what I thought about his "league" comment, but saw that he beat me to it:

> From: CoolJeeves@gmail.com
> To: RazzMaJazz@gmail.com
> Subject: Project Reuniting
>   Auntie K. with Dr. B.
>
> Hey, Jazz. Here's the info for Dr.
> Babaloo; found it easily in my mom's
> video library. The Charles Westford
> dude must be his agent or manager:
> Dr. Babaloo Bains, c/o Mr. Charles
> Westford, Suite 12-E, Oxford Square,
> London, WC1X 9HX U.K.

Sorry about the Tyler R. comment.
None of my biz.

Jeeves had to be the only guy on the planet who wrote his emails properly, with capitals and correct grammar and punctuation.

And darn right it was none of his biz! He may have been right about me not being in Tyler R.'s league, but I didn't need to be *told*.

Once I finished huffing and hissing about the (okay, maybe it *is* true) "league" comment, I started to get totally excited about writing to Dr. Babaloo. I wondered if Auntie Kinder felt the same way around Dr. Babaloo that I felt whenever Tyler R. was near— like an utter doofus with no control over her most basic motor skills.

It was almost like that romance novel I read a while back . . . what was it again? Oh, yeah: *Love's Sweet Dagger*. Except the doctor in that one was a neuro-surgeon who was addicted to narcotics and injected them into the heels of his feet. I prayed that Dr. Babaloo wasn't a heroine junkie or coke-head. All Auntie Kinder needed after finally getting away from her psycho ex-husband was a drug-injecting celebrity doctor.

I didn't want to sound too dorky, and I definitely didn't want to make Auntie Kinder seem desperate, so I tried to make the email casual and matter-of-fact, but with enough subtext and undertone that he could easily read between the lines, if he was looking. No easy task, let me tell you.

~~Dear Dr. Babaloo Bains,~~

~~You don't know me, but I know you~~

~~Dear Dr. Bains,~~

~~Many years ago, you were caught making out (or more) with~~

~~Dear Dr. B,~~

~~What's up?~~

After a couple of hours of searching for the right words, composing, writing, trashing, and re-writing, I finally had my letter.

Dear Dr. Babaloo,

I am the producer of a television show called "Bridging the Gap" on New York City's local public broadcasting station. We would like to interview you on our show about the generation and culture gap between immigrants and their children.

As a public television station, we, unfortunately, can not provide air fare or accommodations, as I am sure you are accustomed to, but we can provide exposure of your very important work to an American audience. . . .

Okay, I know what you're thinking. But in my defense, most of what I wrote in the letter was not too far from the truth.

Mary *was* a production assistant last summer for Channel 23, a local TV station that broadcasted from her college campus (before she dropped out to "find" herself) in New York City: true.

We could *not* provide air fare or pay for accommodations: true.

We could definitely expose Dr. Babaloo to an American audience—me, Cindy, Mary, Toni, Jeeves, and most importantly, Auntie Kinder were, indeed, an American audience: true.

All of this was definitely possible: true/false.

If we (and I did mean *we*, even though I was the only part of "we" who knew about this plan so far) could find cameras, get a place to put them (like a studio), and get to New York City, this plan would totally rock.

And of course, all of this was *if* Dr. Babaloo actually received and read my letter. I knew the chances of that were slim to none, so I didn't think much of sealing the envelope, addressing it, and walking across the street in my flip-flops to drop my little letter in the mailbox. I would move on to another plan tomorrow.

Then I walked back upstairs to my room and picked up *Love's Wayward Journey.*

"What?" I said to cover-girl Charlotte's accusing face. "It's no big deal, okay? Nobody reads those letters, anyway. Besides, he probably gets a ton of fan mail and letters from people wanting him to solve their problems. . . ."

I put the novel back in its hiding spot between the bed frame and mattress before any more niggling doubts could eat away at my brain. Then I worked on Latin, calculus and physics homework until my mom came home and the house sighed with the smells of sizzling cumin, onions, and ginger.

Chapter 9

After dinner, I was on the phone with Mit, on one of our weekly phone calls. My mom always hovered upstairs for the first few minutes, pretending to make her (already-made) bed, before giving me a grin and a thumbs-up, and heading back downstairs.

"My life is misery," I complained, after I heard the last stair creak downstairs.

"Oh, stop," Mit said, lowering some depressing-sounding music. "How could it be? You have *me* in it."

"True. But I want *love*, Mit. Everyone else seems to get to have it, but not me. *Whyyyyy*?" I whined, getting all nasally.

I heard him sigh on the other end. "Jazzy. You need to stop whining and go and do something about it."

"And *what*, exactly, would you suggest I do?"

"This guy you're always talking about—Tyler R. Go *get* him!"

"Excuse me? He is not a promotional pair of underwear at Victoria's Secret that I can just go and 'get.'"

"No, but you have to be proactive, Jazzy. How do you think I get all the boys to fawn over me all the time? I don't just sit around whining, you know." He'd taken to calling me Jazzy, which I actually didn't mind so much.

"So what should I do? Slam him against a locker and shove my tongue in his mouth?"

"Oooooh, listen to you! G'ahead, getcho freak on." He laughed. "No, seriously. Look at the girls he's into, then *compete*. Blow them out of the water. You're in that special program, right? Aren't you used to competing and coming out on top? Go do your thang."

When we hung up, I mulled over his words. He had a point. I thought about the girls I'd last seen Tyler gazing at. They were all different. But the things they had in common were the very things my parents did not allow me to do: cut my hair and wear makeup. Oh, and not to mention *date*. The other things they had in common were also grounds for homicide in the Dhatt house: super-tight jeans and T-shirts, super-short skirts, super-high heels, and other such super-"immodest" items—wayyy out of the question.

Forget it. There was no way. Maybe when the sun started to rotate around the earth. Maybe *then* I could be the kind of girl a guy like Tyler R. might be interested in. Until then, I would just have to accept that I was out of his league.

Jeeves was right, I thought miserably.

What's even worse is that the next morning, Tyler R., himself, totally confirmed it.

He openly stared at me as I walked into the school.

I, like, totally *levitated*.

He pointed to my head in surprise. "Hey, did you get your hair cut? It looks good."

After I almost exploded from hearing Tyler R. tell me I looked good, my feet sort of crash-landed to the ground.

I walked around the corner and took the band out of my hair, letting it fall out of its ponytail. I felt like a liar—like I was misrepresenting myself or something. I hadn't cut my hair; I had just put it back that morning because it was greasy and dull from not being washed. I was still me—same old, boring me.

But Tyler R.'s words reverberated in my brain: *Hey, did you get your hair cut? It looks good.*

I spent the rest of the day not focusing on anything my teachers were saying, and feeling like I had *World's Biggest Loser* tattooed on a hidden spot on my body. I knew it was there, but no one else did. And no one else cared. I was the only one who knew how much it sucked to be me.

I couldn't think of anything else but my hair all day. It became so huge in my mind, that it wasn't just my hair any more. It was everything I wasn't allowed to do and want. It was always supposed to be in order. Neat. Perfect. Obedient. Just laying there, quietly, harnessed in a ponytail.

At the end of the day—as I was staring into my locker for something like three hours, not wanting to go home, do homework, and be "genius," FSL Jazz, who had no life and no hope of ever having a boyfriend, and parents who were going to tailor my life to suit *their* needs—something clicked.

And that's when it hit me: Thursday mornings, Cindy had a free period first thing. I would miss French, but I wasn't too worried about that—not to sound conceited or anything, but I always aced languages.

The next morning, after my mom left for work around six, I called Cindy. I knew Ms. Reda would already be at the salon, and Mary and Toni would still be home because they usually rolled in a little later.

Cindy's phone rang four times, then went through to voice mail.

"Cin—it's me. I'm calling right back. *Pick up*, it's important!"

I called back and it rang once, then went through to voice mail again. She must have been checking the message I left.

I hung up and redialed again.

"*What?*" she said, her annoyance scarcely concealed.

"Sorry for waking you, Cin. Get up, I'm coming over."

"What's going on?"

"I'll tell you when I get there. Are Mare and Toni there?" She paused. I heard rustling, so I knew she was getting out of bed. Then, "No. Mare slept at a friend's last night, and you know Toni got her own place last year after she graduated from college. But I'll call them if it's that important."

"It is," I said quickly.

"This better be good, Jazz."

I quickly brushed my teeth, grabbed my backpack and practically ran the three blocks to her house.

She opened the door before I reached for the doorbell. "What's going on?" she asked, her brow furrowing in concern.

I followed her in, dropped my backpack and took a deep breath. "I want a makeover," I announced, before I could change my mind.

Her eyes widened. "What *kind* of makeover?"

I nodded vigorously. "The works," I said breathlessly. "Everything."

Her hands flew up to cover her mouth. "Mare is gonna *love* this."

Then she rushed around getting their living room set up as a salon. She lay down a tarp, brought over a kitchen chair and piled it with cushions, pulled out a set of scissors, thinning shears, comb, spritzer bottle, and a whole bunch of other instruments. I watched and helped while a million dragonflies did nosedives in my stomach.

Just as we were trying on different shades of foundation, Mary and Toni walked in.

Mary took one look at the living-room-turned-salon and stopped in her tracks. "Wait. What's going on?"

Cindy grinned. "We're, um, jazzing Jazz up."

Mary threw her arms up. "Finally! I *told* you a little makeup wouldn't hurt. Your mom finally came around, huh?" She walked over to me and tilted my chin up with one finger. I could see her imagining the possibilities the way she did customers at the salon.

"Wellll. . . ."

Toni groaned. "Oh, no."

Mary grinned. "Hey, you gotta do what you gotta do." She pointed to one of the three shades Cindy had rubbed onto my cheek. "This one."

"Jazz wants a *total* makeover," Cindy said.

Toni dropped into a nearby chair. "What kind of total?"

Mary looked me in the eyes. "Total . . . as in hair, too?"

I clenched my fists under the black plastic tent Cindy had me wrapped in and nodded once, firmly. "Total as in hair." Then I added, "Just a teensy bit."

"You are *so* going to be in royal doo-doo," Mary said matter-of-factly. "Didn't you say that was against your religion?"

Toni's eyes brightened. "Awesome! *Viva la revolución*, girl," she said, throwing a fist in the air.

"It is," I said to Mary, "but as Toni so kindly pointed out, my dad's hair is cut. How tough can they be with me?" I paused, then added, ". . . Um, but could we still make it, like, you know, subtle?"

"So a cut that could pass for a non-cut," Cindy explained.

I sighed. "Can we please get on with it before I chicken out?"

Toni grinned and stood up. "Gimme those scissors."

About ninety minutes later, I stood in front of Cindy's dresser mirror. I was utterly speechless. Mary, Cindy and Toni stood around me, staring at my new look.

"Wow, you look horrified, Jazz!" Cindy said, stroking my shoulder.

"It'll grow back," Mary added. "Before you know it, it'll be almost as long as it was before."

"I guess I kind of got carried away with the scissors," Toni said apologetically. "But you have such great cheekbones! It would be a crying shame to keep them hidden behind all that hair."

I shook my head, and fringes of shiny black hair danced around my eyes. Toni had given me bangs, and layered the sides into long fringes that swayed against the sides of my face, pointing to my cheekbones and eyebrows and lips.

Mary had tweezed and waxed my brows into a shape that was scientifically and mathematically calculated with the use of a measuring instrument and tracing paper, as well as waxed the tiny fuzz above my upper lip. These two small acts made my eyes pop out and my lips look much fuller.

Finally, Cindy had finished it all off with some subtle lipstick and eye makeup. I'd decided that foundation wasn't really my thing—it felt like a face glove. *Not* comfortable.

"I'm not horrified," I said, astonished. "I'm *hot*."

There was some mini-celebrating and sashaying of the hips, then Mary and Toni left after a long hugging session and lots of cooing and praising about my new look.

Mary said, "Go get 'em, Jazz! They won't know what hit them."

Toni enveloped me for about an hour before holding me out and whispering, "You have to be strong, now. You're about to go *through* it, babes."

Cindy and I walked to school and I swear I was floating about two feet higher than her. I couldn't believe I could look like this! I was actually hot. *Me!*

Cindy was positively gushing about seventy words per second. "I can't believe what a difference! Who knew what a couple of snips in the right places could do for you! You really have gorgeous hair, Jazz—omigosh, I would *kill* for hair that thick and straight. And with the bangs, and those eyebrows, we can see how striking your eyes are!"

Gorgeous! Striking!

I couldn't keep my eyes away from all reflective surfaces. I had the unsettling feeling that anyone looking at me from the outside would see just another girl obsessed with her looks, not a Future Star and Leader. Suddenly, I felt a kinship with every hoochie and bindi-bo who ever stopped to fix something at a reflective pit stop.

The rest of the morning was one surreal moment fading into the next. First weird moment of the day: Winston Jones, who I've known since middle school, introduces himself to me and asks if I'm new to the school. He then asks where I've been all his life.

Weird moment number two: Ms. Schiff compliments me on my new "hairdo." This might not seem that weird, but believe me, anyone complimenting my hair was an unusual, extraordinary event.

Weird moment number three: Jeevan Sahota stops dead in his tracks as he's about to pass me in the hall. "Whoa," he says, his face the very definition of confusion. "Is that you, Jazz? You look, um, well . . . *awesome.*"

He looked like he wanted to say more, but I was not in the mood to answer questions that could possibly put a damper on how amazing I was feeling. And I can not overstate how very, very weird it was to have Jeeves look at me the way he looked at some of the bindi-bos.

I had Cindy take a picture of me with her cell phone and send it to Mit.

He texted back immediately: *OMG! Top-model material!!*

I swelled up with something like pride and pleasure. I totally floated on cloud nine thousand all day, hoping to see Tyler R. I sat on the outside edge of our usual row in the cafeteria, I took a seat near the door in all my classes, and I lingered around his locker and in the halls between classes. But no Tyler R. That was the only slow, pinprick leak in my bursting balloon of joy.

When I walked over to Auntie Kinder's, Pammi opened the door before I rang the buzzer.

"Hey," I said.

"Ho-ly! LOOK AT YOUR HAIR."

I reached up and gingerly touched my new hair. "You like?"

"*Your parents are going to kill you!*"

"You can quit shouting, Pams," I said, walking past her.

"YOUR PARENTS ARE GOING TO KILL YOU."

"Will you stop saying that?! And shut the door, okay? The entire floor'll be out in a sec."

"There is NO way you can hide that," Pammi said, closing the door. "What're you going to do?"

The euphoria of being at school and getting all kinds of compliments from teachers and students, and Cindy and her sisters, was starting to give way to a kind of dread. It had started on the walk to Auntie Kinder's. "I don't know, Pams. It really seemed like a good idea at the time. I was hoping your mom might have some suggestions. I'm sure she did things her parents weren't thrilled about when she was my age. . . ."

She shook her head and stared at me, giving me glances which were a mixture of shock and awe, until Auntie Kinder came home.

Auntie Kinder took one look at me and dropped her jaw. "Goodness," she breathed. Then she pursed her mouth. "Clearly your parents have not seen this yet because you are still *alive.*"

Suddenly, I freaked. Like, all of a sudden, cold, bony fingers were squeezing my stomach. I dropped back onto the pile of large, sequined pillows I'd been sitting on. "Auntie Kinder, I'm scared to go home!" I moaned.

Pammi shook her head again. "I *told* you your parents are going to kill you."

Auntie Kinder flashed her a look, then turned to me. "You *ought* to be scared. You know exactly how your parents will feel about this flagrant transgression." She slipped her shoes off and plopped into a kitchen chair.

"That bad?" I asked.

"Welll . . . in some ways your parents are extremely traditional," she said, "but in others, they're surprisingly open-minded. I hope for your sake, this time they'll be the latter."

"I'm Sikh," I wailed, like it was news. "We're not supposed to remove a single hair on our bodies—unless we're male."

She threw back her head and let out a tired laugh. "I'm Sikh, too, love, and there are many, many men who do keep their hair, in spite of the prevailing attitudes wherever they might live. But, yes—you're right. I believe it's written into the scriptures somewhere that sometimes it's okay if men cut their hair but it's never okay for women and girls."

"This is not funny!" I cried.

She sighed. "Sweet child," she said, suddenly looking older than I'd ever seen her, "I gave the same argument when I was younger, but it makes no difference. You know it's not the same. They'll simply tell you men should keep their hair, too, but it's harder to find a job as a man with a turban, that there's more discrimination and more risk for men when they stand out."

I slumped against the chair. "So there's nothing you can do to help me with this?"

She smiled apologetically. "Sorry, Jazz. You walked into this with your eyes wide open when you chopped all that lovely, thick hair off. You put your shoe right square in the doggy pile, and you must clean it up, darling."

Hurricane-sized chaos blasted through our home that night. And now, two weeks later, my mother was still not talking to me. I actually preferred this to the trauma of the moment she first saw my hair—when she wept and pumped her fist in the air, asking all ten gurus for their mercy and compassion:

"*Hiyo Rubba!* Such an insolent girl! What must I have done in a past life to deserve this?"

"Mom, it's just a haircut," I'd pleaded. It had seemed like such a good idea at the time.

She fell into a dining chair, clutching her chest. "Just a haircut! JUST a haircut!"

My eyes stung. "Why is it such a big deal?"

She glared at me. "We do *not* take scissors to our hair. Each hair on our bodies is sacred! Numbered by the Almighty! God placed each and every hair on our bodies with purpose, Jassy. Removing any of the hairs shows *utter* disregard for His wisdom. How will anyone know you're a Sikh girl if you have no hair?"

"Daddy cuts his hair," I argued. "And you shave your armpits, and everyone still knows we're Sikh."

Her mouth thinned into a line. "That's different."

"Why?" I dug in. "How is it any different?"

She inhaled sharply. "Because I'm married and your father is a man."

"That makes *no* sense!"

"I'm married," she said calmly, her nostrils flaring. "Any alterations or beautification *I* do is for my husband, within the sanctity of marriage. A young girl like you, unmarried, working hard to look appealing to boys could be twisted into something very unpleasant! And your father—he is a man."

"So it's not about God and the Almighty, then! It's about what people will say and *think* about me."

"About us! About the whole of our family! It is a reputation, a family's honor we are talking about, Jassy, not simple, ordinary gossip!"

Her voice was like thunderclaps, and I actually began to slowly back away.

"The looks people give, nasty comments . . . these can make life very difficult to live, Jassy," she continued, losing no steam. "You are too young and arrogant to understand! If you wander around with shorn hair and makeup, you appear wild, insolent, and people make assumptions about your character! And what will Gurmit's parents think? Have you thought of that?"

Then, suddenly, her expression changed. "*Beta*," she said in a gentler tone, "I know you want to look nice for Gurmit. He is a handsome boy. But you must still remain simple and modest before your wedding. People will talk, otherwise, *heh-na*?"

A peal of laughter burst out of my mouth before I could stop myself.

Her eyes flashed. "Jassy, that is enough. We have been too lenient with you! You've been spoiled with all this freedom."

She closed her eyes for a moment and took a deep breath. I had the distinct feeling that if she hadn't done that, she might've lost all control and flung the nearest heavy object my way.

When she opened her eyes, she began again, in a quieter, calmer voice. "This time," she said, "you will receive a proper punishment: You are not to work at Cindy's mother's salon until your father and I decide it's okay. You will not use the telephone, including your cell phone. School and home—that is *all*, until your father and I decide otherwise."

My eyes began to sting. "Ha! That should be easy, then. How is that any different from my life as usual?"

"Enough! This is what you learn in your brilliant, genius, FSL classes? To talk back to your parents, to be rude and disrespectful?"

I swallowed hard and ran past her, up the stairs to my bedroom, where I tried to write and read and surf the Net—anything to keep myself from thinking about how interminably long this punishment was going to feel.

I hadn't even been allowed to go to Auntie Kinder's. My mom carefully explained to Mit's mom that our weekly phone chats would have to be put on hold for a bit because I was "on punishment," and she had steadily and diligently given me the silent treatment.

Although home was a bit like being in a hole in those two weeks, school was another story. I'd taken to putting on a nice shade of shimmering, Mocha Sunset lipstick and coordinating eye shadow (courtesy of Mary) when I hit school grounds. The one wildly HUGE payoff? Tyler R. finally saw my new "look" a week-and-a-half into my punishment. And—*ding-ding-ding!*—it totally had the desired effect.

He was hanging out against the windows looking over the courtyard. Instead of his usual nod, he stared at me, unflinching, and turned his head to keep staring as I walked by.

Suddenly, the skimpy, lacy tank top I'd borrowed from Cindy—and changed into in the bathroom because my mother would have a conniption if she saw me in it in public—seemed like the *best* idea I'd ever had in my life.

"Hey," he said, jogging to catch up with me, "Jazz, right?"

I nodded. "Hi." At least I hope I said hi. It might have been "Hrmphi."

He ran a finger through my hair, gently gliding through a few strands. "You look great, Jazz."

I stopped walking and turned to face him.

His eyes glimmered as he took a step closer to me. "I almost didn't recognize you."

Breathe, Jazz, breathe.

Then he gave that little teasing smile and started walking backwards, still looking at me. "I'll *definitely* see you later, Baby J."

I stood still and held my breath until he turned back around.

As I began to breathe again and walked slowly to class, I noticed the looks I was getting from the people around me. A few of the hoochies had their lips stretched into plastic smiles and a couple of jocks had hooded, interested looks in their eyes. Apparently, talking to Tyler R. *while he ran a finger through your hair* was of great public interest –at least in the hall. And it seemed to—suddenly—turn me into a person people noticed . . . people my age, not just teachers and parents and school officials.

That was a very, very good day. And it got better after I got home.

"Jassy."

A jolt zinged through me at the sound of my mother's voice calling my name. A couple of weeks ago, she was searing it into my ears with the fires of fury.

I cleared my throat. "Um, yeah?"

"Come in here, please."

I put my backpack down and walked into the kitchen, trying to keep my knees from quaking too hard.

"Sit down," she said, motioning to a kitchen chair.

I sat down, preparing myself for what might come next.

"Jassy, Daddy and I have talked about this matter in depth," she began, "and we agree that what you did was completely unacceptable."

I gritted my teeth.

"However, it was not unforgivable. You are no longer under punishment, but you must agree to discuss all decisions, especially regarding your appearance with us."

I swallowed hard, thanking God, the Goddess, Allah, Krishna, Jesus, Buddha, and science that I remembered to wash my face in the girls' bathroom after last period.

"This is very important, *beta*. You are a girl, and you are our responsibility until you are married. It is our duty to make sure nothing happens to you until you are safely in your new home with your new in-laws. Understand?"

I nodded. *Anything* to get out of being grounded.

"Good," she said. "Here is your cell phone—for emergencies only, *heh-na*?" She slid it across the table to me.

I nodded again. "Does this mean I can work at Redalicious this Saturday?"

She heaved herself up from the chair. "Yes. But straight home afterwards."

Hallelujah! Not wanting to shift the vibe in the room, and my mother's mood, I delicately picked up my cell phone and ran up the stairs.

Chapter 10

"It's so sad that anything love and romance-related has to be kept under strict secrecy in my house," I said, lying on my bed. I cradled the phone against my shoulder.

"That's the way it is in all our homes, Jazzy," Mit said.

"You mean all brown homes."

"No," he said slowly, "I mean *all* homes. Apparently, whoever we pick as an intimate partner is cause for national concern when we pick the 'wrong' person."

I sighed. "True."

It was Sunday, and we were catching up since my grounding. I'd sent him a few quick texts and emails when my mom thought I was doing homework, but talking on the phone was so much better.

I learned that he actually had a lot to do with my being ungrounded. Mit had shown his mom the picture Cindy sent him from her cell phone. His mom thought I looked "lovely" and called my mom to say so. And that was all it took.

"I still want to get Auntie Kinder together with the former love of her life," I said, switching the phone to my other ear.

He made a sound of agreement. "It is so romantic, the idea of reuniting long-lost lovers." He was as much of a romance addict as I was. Only instead of reading trashy novels, he devoured romantic comedies on TV and DVD.

"I mean, if a passionate and sizzling affair with Tyler R. is out of the question for a girl in my predicament, how amazing would it be to have that love and romance close enough that I could live vicariously?"

"A passionate and sizzling love affair with Tyler R., or any boy, is *never* out of the question, Jazzy."

"It is if you have my parents. I know my parents love each other, but they never *pined* for one another, y'know? They met, like, a month before their *wedding* night, or something. Auntie Kinder and Dr. Babaloo should have been together, but were *kept* apart."

"I bet your parents pined after *someone* in their lives. Maybe not each other, but I'll bet anything they did some pining."

"Dude. Ew. They did not."

"Speaking of pining, mine is over."

"NO. You finally made a move on Ken?" Ken was what we called his latest crush because he looked so much like a Ken doll on steroids. He was a huge football player who had apparently been returning Mit's "looks of interest."

"I *so* did. And we are *all* over each other."

I could hear the excitement in his voice. "Congrats, dude! Wow. Do you *ever* strike out?"

"Not with this bod, baby."

I laughed. "You do have a rad bod."

When we hung up, I went downstairs—actually, *floated* toward smells from the kitchen. Since my mom and dad were both home on Sundays, they took the opportunity to immerse me in Indian-ness.

This Sunday, they had invited the Purewals over for dinner— my cousin, Kamaljit (imagine all the possible conjugations of *that* name), her brother Ranjit (another beaut. I was convinced all Indian names were designed to sound like humiliating English derivations that became weapons of mass destruction in the hands of non-Indian ignoramuses), and their parents.

Camel Purewal was my least favorite cousin. I would normally never make fun of another Punjabi name (because that's also in the Handbook), but I had an intense dislike for Camel because she tried to out-Indian me every chance she got. My parents had a huge list of things she was amazing at, beginning with her perfectly round rotis and the immense depth of her gratitude and respect for elders—something I seemed to be egregiously lacking.

So I had no choice but to put on one of the three salwaar-kameez suits I owned, weave my hair (as much of it as I could, now that it was cut) into one long braid down my back, and practice my Punjabi-without-an-accent before they came over.

The last time they were here, Camel had giggled every time I said roti because, apparently, I said it with an American accent.

Tonight, she was wearing a glittering, banana-yellow salwaar-kameez suit. And, of course, she was in the kitchen, zipping around our mothers while I hovered by the door, waiting for the perfect moment to spring my "I have to study" excuse. I wanted nothing more than to slip upstairs to my room and into the far more interesting lives of Charlotte and Enrique in *Love's Wayward Journey.*

"Kamaljit, why don't you go upstairs with Jassy?"

I narrowed my eyes at my mom, who looked innocently back at me. I gritted my teeth and turned to Camel. "Wanna go upstairs?"

"No, no, Auntie!" she said, ignoring me. *"Teek heh.* I want to stay here and help."

"Go on, Kamaly," her mother said, smiling conspiratorially at my mom. "Deesh and I have grown-women things to discuss."

My mom gave us a warm, melting smile before she *tch-tch'ed* and shooed us both out while Auntie, the resident gossip columnist, hunkered down to shuck peas at the table.

Camel and I trudged upstairs to my room in silence. I had no idea what I could possibly find to talk about with her.

When we got there, she surveyed my bedroom in silence for a minute. I fiddled around with the mouse on my computer.

"So your parents found someone for you," she said, finally.

"Huh?" I looked at her in surprise. "How did you know?"

She gave me a look of utter contempt. "Are you kidding? I know about *all* your accomplishments. You're Jasbir—smart! Brilliant! A whiz! And now you have an amazing husband lined up."

I stared at her. "*Husband?* Noooo. . . . And he's not really—"

"That's alright," she said airily, "I'm sure it must be tough having to be so perfect all the time."

"*Me?* Perfect?" Me? *She* was every parent's poster child for Good Indian Girls! Well, at least she was for *my* parents.

She pursed her lips. "Aren't you pretty much guaranteed a spot in the college of your choice?"

Er. . . . "Yes, but. . . ."

She waited.

I was going to say "That's only because I'm in the FSL program," but realized how asinine that would sound.

She gave me a look, then turned to the keyboard on my computer and blew on the keys. "When was the last time you dusted in here?" she muttered, while tracing a pattern into the layer of dust on my dresser. She looked up and gave me a phony smile. "So, are you excited?"

I shrugged. "Sort of. I'm really hoping Cindy and I end up at the same college, but she really wants to go to—"

"Not that," she snapped. "About getting *married*. Aren't you excited about starting your life? My mom said your fiancé is amazing."

I had the sudden urge to explain everything to her—that things were not as perfect as she might think. "Cam—I mean, Kamal—it's not what you think . . . I mean, it's not as perfect as you think. . . ."

She looked at me and waited, her face hopeful and open. And just for a split second, we had an opportunity to connect. I realized that in another world, a world where parents didn't compare their daughters in some sort of point system where there was a distinct pass and fail component, Camel and I might actually have been friends.

But there was no way I could tell her why things weren't perfect without also telling her the truth about Mit. And that was *so* not an option.

"It's really not that perfect. . . ." I finished lamely.

"Right," she said, getting up and walking to my bookcase. She pulled out an Advanced Psychology text. "So you cut your hair. That must've devastated your parents. Don't you feel awful? I think girls look way better with long hair, anyway." She glanced at me. "No offense. But I think it takes courage to assert your Indian-ness in the west, don't you? I mean anyone can blend in— but not everyone can be different and be okay with it."

Okay, moment of connection over. I quickly remembered why she was my least favorite cousin. Those last couple of lines sounded like they came straight out of the Desi Parent Handbook. I wanted to say, "What takes courage is tolerating your breath," but I kept my mouth shut.

A bombastic clap of laughter rose up from downstairs. Camel's father's voice bellowed above everyone else's. She looked sharply out the door and headed toward the stairs.

"We should get back down to help our mothers," she said, already halfway down the steps.

The rest of the night, I watched her zip around, a flash of banana-yellow with gold sequins, tinkling her delicate laughter, innocently widening those bug eyes, and nodding, acquiescing, consenting.

As the Purewals piled into their car and waved good-bye, I felt a stab of something for Camel. I'd always thought she was a catty beyotch, but tonight I caught a glimpse of something really sad just underneath that brittle shell.

What she'd said about it taking courage to be okay with being different made sense. I knew about being different. I was FSL—different, even among the different. But did it take courage to just keep doing what you were told, without asking any questions? Did it take a different kind of courage to not love the person you loved, and do what was considered appropriate—as Auntie Kinder had done? Or to pretend you were something you weren't—like what Mit was doing?

As I trudged up the stairs to my bedroom, I wondered what turned some girls into Kamaljit Purewals and others into girls like me—ones who started doing things that got them into a whole heap of crap. I wondered if Auntie Kinder had been a girl like me.

And my mom—had she been a Kamal, or a getting-in-deep-doodoo-for-breaking-the-rules Jazz? What about Mrs. Sahota?

If the night had ended there, I would've read some more of *Love's Wayward Journey* until I fell asleep, dreaming about Tyler R.'s bronze-gold pecs. But the night did not end there. What happened next kicked my Auntie Kinder-Dr. Babaloo efforts into URGENT mode.

Auntie Kinder called and came over about twenty minutes after the Purewals left. I heard the door open, then a hurried, almost hysterical-sounding Auntie Kinder. I opened my door and crept to the top of the stairs to listen.

All I could make out was, "Pammi . . . sleeping . . . a friend's. . . ." and then, "He wants to take her, Deesh!"

My fingers tightened on the railing. Mom and Auntie Kinder moved into the kitchen and I walked gingerly down the stairs, though I don't think anyone would've noticed me, anyway. From the sound of Auntie Kinder's voice, and her coming over like this on a Sunday night, I knew something was terribly wrong.

I heard more talking, then my dad's angry, but steady, voice. "Deesh, I'm going to speak to that attorney friend of mine. Don't worry, Kinder."

I watched him slip on his shoes, grab his sweater and rush out the door, jabbing the keys on his cell phone as he jogged down the steps of our porch. Then, I walked slowly into the kitchen. I knew my mother didn't like to share things with me that she thought were too "stressful" or "grown-up." But something was wrong with Auntie Kinder, and possibly Pammi, and I needed to know what it was.

Auntie Kinder was sitting at the kitchen table with her face in her hands. I could hear her sobbing softly.

"What's going on, Mom?" I asked, going immediately to Auntie Kinder's side.

Auntie Kinder didn't look up.

I looked at my mom and she just shook her head in a mixture of sadness and anger. "Don't worry, *beta*, go back upstairs."

Not a chance. "What's the matter? What happened?" Then my heart caught in my throat. Pammi! "Is Pammi okay?"

Auntie Kinder lifted her head up. "Pammi's alright, darling," she said in a strained voice. "It's . . . I'm afraid her father. . . ."

Blood began to pound furiously in my ears.

Auntie Kinder dropped her head into her hands again and my mom stroked her back.

My throat was parched. "Is he here again? What does he want? Why doesn't he leave you guys alone?"

"I don't know." Auntie Kinder's voice was a muffled kind of wail, and it all came rushing out at once now. "Suddenly he wants Pammi in his life again. He hasn't been around for years, Deesh! Now he wants to take my baby from me."

Her voice cracked and my mom put her arms around Auntie Kinder's trembling shoulders. "He can't do that, Kinder," my mom said, with rage simmering just beneath her words. "All idle threats. He wants to get to you through your daughter because he knows that will hurt you the most."

"But an *unfit mother*? How can he claim that?" Her voice choked. "Because I worked nights as a nurse to put my daughter through one of the best girls' schools in the state, I'm an unfit mother?"

I saw my mother's eyes darken in a way I'd never seen before. "We'll talk to this attorney friend of ours. Don't worry. It'll all be fine."

My own eyes burned with unshed tears. I clenched my fists and ran up the stairs to my room. I texted Cindy immediately with what I'd heard.

She texted right back: *OMG, CN HE DO THAT???*

I responded with: *IDK*. Then I paced back and forth next to my bed. I pulled out my cell again and texted: *BUT WE HAV 2 DO SUMTHIN!*

A few seconds later, my phone buzzed. It was a text from Cindy: *TOTALLY!*

The question was what?

Chapter 11

I didn't have to search far for the solution to my Auntie Kinder-Dr. Babaloo reunion situation. It kinda dropped into my lap.

In the weeks following President's Day weekend—the weekend of Auntie Kinder's teary visit—me, Cindy and Mit spent lots of brain and virtual airtime trying to find ways to get Dr. Babaloo and Auntie Kinder together. It was no longer just a romantic fairy tale that would be cool to see turning into a reality. Now, it was about keeping Pammi with her mom, and more importantly, *away* from her dad.

"If Auntie Kinder and Dr. Babaloo were to rekindle their former love," Mit said on the phone, "Pammi would have a more stable home situation. Then that controlling jerk-off wouldn't have a leg to stand on."

When I told Cindy about it during our walk home with Jeeves, she asked, "Could it work in the other direction, though?"

I wrinkled my eyebrows. "What do you mean?"

Jeeves nodded. "I wonder if they could make that into something worse."

I stopped short, his words sinking in. "You mean, imply that she's a skanky ho or something?"

Cindy shrugged. "Who knows? I've seen it happen on TV."

"*Augh.*" I hadn't thought of that.

Jeeves and I took turns hugging Cindy good-bye at her corner, then continued walking.

"Maybe I could try to get Auntie Kinder to go to England, instead of trying to get him here?"

"Dude, there is no way she's going to England now—that's where *he* is," Jeeves said, plucking a pine cone off a tree as we passed a perfectly winter-landscaped lawn. "I could ask my mom if we have any family in England that we could visit. . . ."

"And then what, genius?"

He glared at me. "I don't see *you* doing so well in the brilliant-ideas department."

I kicked a rock. "I know. I'm sorry."

And then today, I came home from school to quite an earth-shattering moment. I mean, my whole brain sort of imploded.

There was a letter addressed to me from a Mr. Charles Westford, which rang no bells. It was from England. You'd think this might have given me a clue. But no.

I opened it up on my way up the stairs, and stumbled at the top step. I fell flat on my face, palms stinging with the slap they made on the hardwood floors.

Dear Ms. Dhatt,

Thank you for contacting us regarding an appearance on "Bridging the Gap." Are you in any way affiliated with Charlie Rose? We do love him!

Nonetheless, Dr. Babaloo is doing a promotional tour through America for his first U.S. book, and he'll be making a stop in New York City. We would be delighted to squeeze a brief interview with your television show into his schedule at that time.

Please contact my assistant, Ms. Ravinder Lally, to make the necessary arrangements.

We look forward to working with you.

Kind Regards,

Mr. Charles Westford.

Um, okay.

What?!?!?!?!?!!

After about three and a half seconds of mulling it over, I was on the phone with Cindy. She and her sisters were at the salon and, lucky for me, it was a slow period with only a few customers.

When I told Cindy about the letter, she hooted, then yelled a summary of what I'd said—and done, since Mary and Toni didn't know about the letter I'd written in the first place—to her sisters. After a short pause, the three of them burst into mini-explosions of laughter for at least a solid five minutes.

"Sure, laugh it up, you guys! *Hilarious*. Ha, ha."

This only started another round of hooting and screeching, during which I put the receiver down twice on my pillow, only to come back and find the laugh-fest hadn't yet subsided.

When they finally stopped cackling, Cindy asked, "So, what're you going to do?"

"You mean, what are *we* going to do?"

"Noooo," she said slowly. "I mean what are *you* going to do?"

"C'mon, Cin! You guys have to help me. . . ."

"Write him back and tell him the truth," Toni called out.

"Am I on speaker?" I asked.

"Of course," all three replied.

"So, what truth shall I tell him? The one that goes: Hey, Dr. Babaloo! I'm sorry to disturb your life, but you know that girl you were making out with in the back seat of a car, like, a million years ago? That girl who then got married off to someone she didn't know? Well, she has a daughter now and the guy she married turned out to be a psycho and now she really needs your help. . . ?"

"Okay, okay—we get it," Toni said.

"You guys," I used my best imploring voice. "This is the second chance at love that Auntie Kinder *deserves*."

"She totally does deserve that," Cindy said, over the sound of running water.

"And what about 'We're talking about love—anything is possible,' Mare?"

"I meant that!" Mary shouted, from what sounded like the bottom of a barrel.

"Toni," I pushed, "wouldn't this be the ultimate 'Take that!' to Auntie Kinder's ex-husband? If she met and re-united with the man that she loved first and *for real*, wouldn't that be the best revenge, ever?"

"It would. . . ." Toni conceded.

"And Mare, weren't you a production assistant last summer on a public television station?"

"Well, yeah, but. . . ."

"C'mon, Mare," I pleaded.

Her voice came closer to the phone—actually her sigh came closer. "Jazz, do you know what a PA does on a set?"

"No," I admitted.

"We get coffee. We sort mail. We run errands. We block off streets from public access. . . . I hardly got close to the actors or cameras or lights, or anything like that."

"Oh," I said, deflated.

Another sigh from someone.

After a pause, Toni said, "Hey, Mare, weren't you pretty close to one of the producers on that show?"

"If you can call a fifty-four-year-old stumpy producer hitting on me 'close,' then, yeah, sure."

"No, not him," Toni said, "some other guy you used to talk about—you said he was cute, and he was a producer or something?"

There was another pause and some shuffling.

I shifted in my spot on the bed, trying not to get too excited about the emerging possibility.

"Oh, wait—Roger? Yeah, he was a cutie, for sure. Twenty-eight, with thick, black, wavy hair. . . ." Her voice drifted off for a moment, then snapped back. "Married, though. Happily. But he was the son of one of the producers, and a producer, himself. Really sweet guy."

"Mare," I said, proceeding carefully. "Do you think Roger might be able to help us?"

"Hmm," she said. Then after a long pause, "Wouldn't hurt to ask, I guess."

"No, it wouldn't!" I said, bouncing up and down. "Thankyouthankyouthankyou, Mare! This could be what gets psycho Mr. Auntie Kinder out of her and Pammi's hair forever! And reunites her with the true love of her life—a TV star!"

"Wow," Cindy breathed. "This could actually happen."

"No," said Toni. "We're going to make it happen. Auntie Kinder is about to kick some ex-husband ass."

"This is exciting!" Mary squealed. "I'm going to call Roger right now—get off the line, Jazz, we'll call you right back."

Apparently, "right back" didn't mean any time today or in the near future. I was texting Cindy and calling Mary incessantly, but she still hadn't heard back from Roger.

I waited, I waxed, I tweezed, I wallowed. Still, no word. I tried to read, then fantasized about Tyler R. But it was all useless. I played games on my computer. I called Cindy, but all we could talk about was how we wished Mary would beep through during our call.

It had been almost a week since Mary told me she was going to call Roger and get "right back" to me. I was beginning to think I would never hear from her again. She wasn't at the salon on Saturday, so I couldn't even pester her. But I did the next best thing—I pestered Cindy. She only said that Mary was "working on it," and if I didn't stop annoying everyone, Mary would call the whole thing off. That got me to stop, but it was like that antsy feeling you get when you're a kid on a long drive—*are we there yet? Now? how about now?* It sucked.

"Hey, Charlotte," I said, pulling out *Love's Wayward Journey.* "Were you scared when you left your dad to go after your One True Love?"

My cell phone buzzed, sending vibrations all through my butt. I'd forgotten it was still in my back pocket. I took it out and checked the ID. It was Mary.

It was *Mary*!

I snapped the phone open.

"I've got neeeews," she sang.

"What, what, *whaaaat*?!"

She giggled. "Hmm, should I just tell her, Toni, or should I make her wait?"

I heard Toni laugh in the background.

I didn't see what was so darn funny. "TELL ME."

"Oh, alright," she said. "I managed to snag. . . ."

"WHAT?!?!?!?! You managed to snag *what*?"

"Oh, relax," she teased, "I managed to snag not only some studio time over . . . let's see—not this weekend, not the next, but the one after that, but a few real, heavy-duty, *pro*-fess-ional TV cameras! And lights, too!" She couldn't keep the squeal out of her voice at the end.

"Wow, that's soon! You are awesome, Mare!" I gushed.

She giggled again. "That's what I keep hearing."

"You are SO the best! I *love* you!"

Her voice sobered. "There is one catch, Jazz."

I was so thrilled that my half-truths were going to pay off in such a big way that I couldn't have cared less.

"Roger was really into Auntie Kinder and Dr. Babaloo's story. He actually wants to shoot the whole thing."

I was not fully comprehending. "Huh?"

"He wants to shoot their reunion, and possibly air it as part of a show in the future."

Suddenly, it dawned on me. In all the frukkus of planning Dr. Babaloo's arrival and the "shoot," I had completely forgotten that we would have to, somehow, get Auntie Kinder to the studio in New York and that, at some point, she would be face to face with this man she hadn't seen since the day they were torn apart and flung in opposite directions. And now, if well-coifed Roger actually wanted to shoot their first meeting since that day, it could be broadcast on public television!

How would Auntie Kinder take that? I was certain that the past couple of Thursdays I'd gone over there to watch Pammi, Auntie Kinder had *not* gone out for "me time." She'd left with papers and documents and that letter from psycho ex's fancy lawyers in London. From eavesdropping on my parents' conversations, I knew that she'd been visiting the attorney they'd recommended.

Even though I had only the best intentions in my heart, I had a strong feeling Auntie Kinder would not be thrilled with what me and the Reda-Rodriguez girls were cooking up. But even so, I was sure she'd thank me for it later—when she rekindled that flame with Dr. Babaloo and they rode off into the sunset, happily ever after. Right?

Charlotte stared at me dubiously from the cover of *Love's Wayward Journey*.

"Don't give me that look," I said, shoving the book under my pillow.

Chapter 12

The following Saturday, my dad was off—lucky me. That meant lots of possibilities for parental ganging up on yours truly.

Dad was home, rested, and in full Dad form: wrestling on the tube non-stop and a bowl of chips/pretzels/Hot Mix in front of him at all times. My mom spent the day cleaning, cooking and freezing everything in serving-size portions for the week ahead, and generally buzzing around me whenever I was in the vicinity.

So I stayed in my room as long as possible, which, when one is adequately loaded with smutty romance novels from the local library, was actually a pleasant way to spend the day.

This weekend, my dad had ordered *Silsila*, a Bollywood classic, for us all to watch after dinner.

Pammi was with us and spent most of the movie cracking up and pointing to the subtitles. "Hey, check it out, Jazz, *'Your lovely ass a rose, my darling.'*" Then she'd fall into a screeching heap as my mother half-heartedly smacked her on the back of the head.

"*Chee-chee*, Pammi—language!"

"But that's what it said, Deesh Auntie—it's not me!"

Mom gave her a look. "It was a mistake in the sub-titling."

Pammi and I kept up a steady commentary, anyway.

Pammi: *My mom says things are censored. They're not allowed to show any kissing.*

Mom: *It's indecent.*

Pammi: *But I thought they were* married*?? They weren't married??*

Me: *Yeah! They weren't married . . . and she's PREGNANT.*

Mom: [SIIIIIIGH. SIIIIIGH.]

Dad: Bas. *Enough, you two.*

Me: *So he's cheating on his wife with his ex-girlfriend.*

Mom: [Glare]

Me and Pammi: [glued to screen, gripping our seats]

Ending—hero chooses wife and marriage vows (Duty) over love.

Mom and Dad: [Satisfied sigh]

Mom: *See where acting selfishly leads?*

Dad: *Yes, DUTY and obligation,* responsibility *. . . these are of the pillars of good character.*

Mom: *We must own this DVD.*

Me and Pammi: *But what about love?*

Dad: *What is this love-shove nonsense?*

"That Amitabh Bachchan is simply dashing—certainly now, but even as a young man . . . simply breathtaking," my mom said as the credits rolled.

Yuck. Watching my mom swoon over an elderly dude was just mortifying.

"Where would that girl be without him to look after her?" She said, shaking her head.

"It's not real, Mom—it's just a movie."

She ignored me. "You know, Kamaljit's parents have a couple of suitable young men lined up for her. I only hope they find someone as perfect as our Gurmit."

Pammi mouthed, *"Gurmit?"*

I made a face. I was not liking where this conversation was heading.

"Jassy, your daddy and I were discussing this . . . and, since you and Gurmit seem to be getting along so well, we thought it best to make things official."

My stomach knotted up. "What do you mean by 'official'?"

"We thought it might be nice to have a sort of party for you two. You know, invite the key family members, that sort of thing." She was glowing.

"Mom, I'm too involved in my studies right now to think about that," I said, hoping my standard excuse would still hold up in a court of my mother's law.

"I understand, *beta*, but this is important. This way, if you should be seen with Gurmit, people will know you are not simply running around like a loose dog. You are legitimately engaged."

"Engaged!" Pammi's eyes were huge. "You're engaged?"

"I am *not* engaged." I turned and gaped at my mom. "I thought this was guided dating?"

"She is engaged to be engaged," my mom said, turning to Pammi.

"Mom!" I shrieked. "He doesn't even *live* here. Who's going to see us together?!"

"Calm down, *beta*. It's standard, and you will have fun."

"Mom!" I shrieked again. "I'm *seventeen*!"

She looked at me in dismay. "I was almost engaged at your age."

"That was in *India*, Mom! Here, you could be arrested for what you're suggesting."

Her eyebrows shot up. "Arrested? For dating a nice, young boy? Then all of America's teenagers should be arrested, *heh-na*?"

Did I mention that conversing with my mother was the most exasperating experience since, like, EVER? "I meant for marrying a minor," I said through clenched teeth.

She heaved a sigh for about half an hour. "No one is *marrying* you, Jassy," she said finally, in the same tone she used for Pammi when she was seven. "I was just talking about a party. It would be good practice for the actual engagement party when it happens."

"I'm not ready, Mom. If I want to get into a good college, I need to focus on my *studies* right now. Otherwise they won't let me in."

"Good to focus on studies, Jassy," my dad said, making his way into the kitchen. "How many families are lucky enough to have Superstar and Leadership talent in their own children?"

Thank you!

"This is about *life*, and it is just as important," my mother said, for his benefit. Then to me, "Just think about it, okay? That is all I ask."

I waited—prayed—for a counter-argument from my dad, but all I got was the screen door slamming as he went out into the back yard. Traitor.

"Fine," I said, dropping my shoulders.

My mother's eyes turned into the North Star and Venus, shining huge and globular as she prattled on and on about how mature I was becoming.

I cut her off, walked Pammi out, then muttered something about needing to study, and headed upstairs.

I was doomed. And things were about to go from bad to waaaaay worse.

Monday was one of those days where March decides to give everyone a sneak preview of what things are going to be like when Spring rolls around. Cindy and I decided to eat lunch outside on the bleachers and watch the guys play basketball without their shirts on. There was still snow on the ground, and even though it wasn't warm enough to go shirtless, the guys were working up a sweat. Jeeves was out, of course. He was a permanent fixture on the basketball courts when the weather turned warm. He waved when he saw us.

We had just settled down and taken a couple of bites out of our respective sandwiches when Tyler R. came out. He had a redhead with him who kept giggling and giving him little shoves as they climbed up to a middle row.

Cindy looked at me and wiggled her eyebrows. "There he is, Mr. Super-Hottie of Your Dreams."

"Lord, please help me stay upright," I said, completely losing my appetite. There wasn't much room in my stomach anyway, with all the commotion that was going on in there.

Cindy laughed. "You're a mess."

Tyler R. looked over his shoulder and smiled. I smiled back. The redhead glanced over her shoulder at us, then edged closer to him as she threw her head back, laughing at something she had said.

I continued to take small bites of my sandwich, grateful that Tyler R.'s back was to us.

"Go, Jeeves!" Cindy yelled, as Jeeves did a twirly leap in the air and slammed the ball into the basket.

He grinned and did a peacock-neck sort of move with his head.

If I wasn't so occupied with the fact that Tyler R. was sitting a few rows down from me, I might have noticed all the impressive moves Jeeves was performing on the court. But as it was, my head jolted up when Tyler R. stood up, turned around, and walked up the steps to where Cindy and I sat.

"Hey, Jazz," he said, squinting his eyes against the sun.

I dropped my sandwich into my bag and crumpled the top shut. "Hey," I breathed.

"Hi!" Cindy said, all perky, "I'm Cindy, Jazz's best friend."

"Hey, Cindy, what's up."

She stood up, her half-eaten sandwich in one hand and her lunch bag in the other. "I'll, um, I have to go inside and, ah, get something from my locker, Jazz. I'll be right back." Then she waved and bounced down the steps, giving me an *eeeeeeeeek!* look as soon as she was out of Tyler R.'s sight.

He sat down next to me and leaned back against the railing. "Is this your usual lunch period?"

I nodded.

"Nice out, right?"

"Mmhm."

We sat in silence for several moments.

"You don't talk much, do you, Baby J.?"

"It's Jazz."

He raised an eyebrow and curved one half of his mouth. "Okay. *Jazz*," he said, leaning reallyreallyreally close. "What else?"

Oh, dear. At this rate, I could *totally* get used to "Baby J." or anything else he wanted to call me. "Well . . . I'm in the FSL program." Brilliant, Jazz. Way to be sexy.

"I know," he said, leaning back again. "I've seen your name in the newsletter. Your friend, Cindy . . . she's in it, too, right?"

I nodded in surprise. I didn't think anyone paid attention to that newsletter.

He laughed. "I'm new, remember? This is one of my ways of learning about the school and who's who."

"Who's who?"

He nodded and looked onto the basketball court. "You know—everyone who's anyone."

I looked onto the court. Jeeves wasn't playing anymore, he was sitting on a bench with his shirt back on. He had a drink in one hand and a towel around the back of his neck. He was watching my exchange with Tyler R. intently.

I shifted uneasily.

"Where are you from, Jazz?"

I hated the *What are you?* and *Where are you from?* questions. To the *What are you?* question, my answer was usually "Annoyed," or "None of your biz-nass." And to the *Where are you from?* I'd answer with something like, "The moon" or "Ur-anus." Okay, maybe not out loud, but that's what I'd be thinking.

But to Tyler, I just said, "My parents were born in India."

"Mmm," he said. Something flickered in his eyes, but he looked out onto the court.

"You're from Trinidad, right?"

He nodded, still not looking at me. For several moments, I wondered if I'd said something wrong. I sat there internally combusting while Tyler R.'s thigh rested lightly against my knee.

"You know," he said quietly, still watching the game on the court. "My dad always says Indians think they're better than West Indians."

I felt my face flame up. "Why?" I swallowed, though there was nothing to swallow—my mouth had dried up like the cranberries my mom once put in her rice by mistake.

He leaned over the side railing and spit his gum out. "He says you think you're more Indian than we are . . . like you're the *real* Indians or something, and we're just pretending."

"I feel like that with my cousin sometimes," I said.

He looked at me.

"Um—like I'm not really Indian enough."

He looked at me for another moment, then threw back his head and laughed.

OMG, I almost *died*. That laugh was like a drug. When he stopped laughing and looked back at me, I went on auto pilot. "Most of the time, I don't think *I'm* a 'real' Indian. And if you asked my parents, they'd probably agree. In fact, every time they think I've forgotten who I am, or that I am, in fact *Indian*, and not American, they threaten to send me back 'home' so that I can get in touch with my roots. Even my Sikhness is questionable these days. . . ."

Zero to verbal diarrhea in zero point three seconds. I bit my tongue to keep from saying anything more.

He looked a little caught off guard for a second. But only for a tiny second. Then he laughed again and put an arm around my shoulders.

HE PUT AN ARM AROUND MY SHOULDERS.

I could barely hear him through the blood pounding in my ears when he said, "You want to go for a walk?"

"Oh," I said, almost dissolving in relief—maybe he didn't think I was a *complete* moron if he wanted to spend more time with me. I turned to look at the doors of the cafeteria. "Cindy's probably going to come back soon."

He looked at the doors, too. "She's been gone for a while. She probably got caught up in something else." He smiled and leaned into my ear. "Come on, Baby J., let's go."

This time I didn't bother to correct him. His *Baby J.* made my legs tremble. I picked up my paper-bag lunch and, keeping my eyes strictly averted from the basketball court, followed Tyler R. down the bleacher steps.

We walked off school property. He seemed to know where he was going and I followed, like those cartoons where people follow the smell of food. We ended up in a small parkette not far from the school.

"I didn't even know this was here," I said, sitting down next to him on a wooden bench.

He leaned down and plucked a yellow marigold that had been planted near the bench and handed it to me. "For you. My parents use these in garlands and for *puja*. Do yours?"

"Um, we're not Hindu," I reminded him. I brought the flower to my nose. "I'm Sikh."

Okay, dude, I know it's totally cheesy, but that marigold was, like, the BEST-SMELLING FLOWER ever in the history of the world.

He nodded and looked around. "I like it here because there's never anyone around. It's like my own private spot."

"It's nice. Do you come here to think?" I have no idea if what I said was audible because all I could hear was the pounding pulse in my ears.

He looked off into the cluster of trees in front of us and curled that one half of his mouth. "Something like that."

Duh, Jazz, I'm sure you're not the only girl he's hung out with here? My face burned as I listened to the birds chirp around me.

"Look," he said, pointing. "The sun and moon are out at the same time." He smiled.

I looked and saw the white half-moon dangling against the pale blue of the sky. It was something I'd seen plenty of times, but never really *looked* at. "I never thought of it that way," I said quietly. "Like, in the daytime, I don't even think of the sun as being *out*, you know?"

He nodded. "The ancient Indians—your people. . . ." he said.

"And yours," I added.

Something shifted in his eyes and he moved closer to me on the bench. ". . . They used to say that when one sun set, a thousand took its place."

I could feel the puffs of his breath dusting my lips. "And that means. . . ?"

"Kiss me, Jazz," he whispered.

I was going to die. Right there in the parkette. My heart was pounding so hard, it was going to rip out of my shirt and flop around on the ground like a fish.

His mouth was warm. He kissed me slowly, ending one kiss and starting up another right after. No tongue. We kissed like that for a long, long time. It was kind of amazing. I'd really only kissed one guy before this—Marcus Leonard. But that was *nothing* like this.

This turned everything liquid inside me. It made me feel beautiful and special and important and . . . *wanted*. I didn't know how else to explain it. When Tyler kissed me, it was almost like I got to see a part of myself reflected under different light. I got to see a part of me I hadn't ever seen before. It was addictive.

When he stopped, he leaned back and murmured, "That was nice, Baby J."

Baby J. I *loved* the way he called me that. I wondered what documents one has to file to have one's name officially changed to Baby J.

His knuckle grazed the back of my cheek, then he stood up and offered me his hand. "I guess we should head back. You ready?"

Um, no. "Sure," I said, slipping my fingers into his. There were flames licking up through my wrists and elbows, right up into my neck.

When we neared school property, he slid my hand out of his and put it around the back of my neck, pulling me close. He kissed me again, a little more pressure this time.

When he let go, he started to walk away slowly. "I've got to take care of something," he said.

I nodded, unable to make my brain send the "walk" signal to my feet.

"Oh," he said, turning back.

Gusts of wind blew into my sails—huge hurricanes—as trumpets echoed inside my head.

"Lemme get your cell number."

I pulled out my cell phone and we keyed in each other's numbers.

He kissed me quickly on the cheek. "I'll see you again, soon, Baby J." And he was gone.

I walked back into the school in a daze, with a stupid grin on my face.

Cindy took one look at me and slapped her hand over her mouth. "Omigosh," she said, reaching out to lightly touch the marigold I'd now threaded through my hair. "*What* happened?"

I couldn't stop grinning. "I am totally in love. I kissed Tyler."

Her jaw dropped. "You got de-virgin-ated!"

I dropped my ear to my shoulder and gave her a look. "I've been kissed before."

"Your mom doesn't count."

"John Lee in second grade. Marcus Leonard in sixth."

"I rest my case." She grabbed my hand and dragged me into a bathroom. "Okay, details, Jazz. *Now*. You have a minute and a half. Go."

I shook my head. "He is *so* amazing, Cin."

She snapped her fingers. "What *happened*?"

"We kissed. And we talked about the stars and the ancient Indians. And for a long time, we just . . . kissed. But it was so . . . warm and sweet and, and. . . ."

"Hot."

I nodded. "Totally hot."

She sighed and leaned against the wall. "I love those kisses."

I decided that I loved them, too.

"What next?"

"I don't know. We didn't talk about it."

"Girrrl! Do I have to school you on *everything*? First the makeup and hair, and now this?"

I nodded, the stupid grin coming back. "I'm about to get schooled, for sure."

After school that day, Cindy and Wes took off to do who-knows-what, so I ended up walking home with Jeeves again. He was unusually quiet and monosyllabic.

"What's up, Jeeves?" I asked.

He shrugged. "Nothin'."

We walked in silence for a few moments.

"I saw you talking to Tyler R. at lunch," he said, looking straight ahead.

A warmth crept up my neck. I nodded.

We fell silent for another couple minutes.

"Be careful, Jazz. You and Tyler R. are not in the same category."

"What the—!" I whirled around to face him. "You said that once to me already. Do you really think I'm *that* hideous that no one like Tyler R. could ever be interested in me?"

His eyes widened in surprise, then he shook his head. "You've got it all wrong, Jazz. That's not what I meant at all."

I ground my teeth. "Then what *did* you mean?"

He shook his head again. "Never mind. Just be careful, that's all."

"Is it because he's popular and gorgeous and I'm not? Or do you think I need to be with an FSL geek? Is that it?"

He winced. "I said never mind."

I stomped along next to him for the rest of the walk until we got to his driveway. "You're an academic snob, Sahota."

He shoved his hands deep into his pockets and dropped his head back to look up at the sky. "It's not about that. I just meant be careful, that's all. With your parents and their views—"

"Do you have to remind me?" I said, clenching my hands into fists. "I live with their freaking views! I get reminded almost on a daily basis that I can't want anything or any*one*, that I'm not allowed to fall in love, I can't want to look nice, I can't go out with my friends—" I stopped just short of the dam bursting and took a deep, quivering breath in.

"Jazz. . . ."

I shook my head and took off toward my house.

Chapter 13

That Thursday, as I hung out with Pammi after school, I knew that when Auntie Kinder came home I had to seize the opportunity. I had to ask her . . . something. I had no clue what I would say to get her to New York City for a weekend with me, my best friend, her sisters, and maybe Roger. Let's not even get into the *reasons* for the trip.

"What is up with you?" Pammi asked at least fifty-nine times.

And when I replied, "Nothing," in what I thought was a nonchalant tone, she rolled her eyes and went back to doing her crossword puzzle.

When she finally arrived, Auntie Kinder plodded into the kitchen looking tired and a little haggard. She pulled out a box from the bakery two blocks down and took out a gorgeous piece of red velvet cake. She cut a slice for Pammi, one for me, and was about to cut another when I held up a hand.

"Uh, none for me, thanks," I said. My stomach was way too jumpy to handle food right now.

I waited until Pammi left the room to do her homework which—and I knew this as a fellow geek—she would become absorbed in for a while.

"Um, Auntie Kinder?" I began, as she sank into a spot on the sofa next to me.

She plunked into a chair, put her feet up on the upholstered footstool in front of her, and popped a forkful of cake into her mouth. She closed her eyes and leaned her head back. "Mmhm?"

I paused. "You look exhausted."

She opened her eyes and set them wearily on me. "I am, Jazz. A lot is going on right now. I feel as if I'm burning the proverbial candle at both ends."

I didn't know how to quite broach the whole thing, so I opted for the direct approach. "So . . . do you like New York City?"

She had closed her eyes to enjoy every last morsel of the last bite of cake, but now she opened one eye. "Sure. It's a great city. Bit dirty, but yes—exciting."

"Wellll," I said, proceeding with caution. "Cindy and her sisters are planning a trip there next weekend. . . ." I trailed off.

"Oh, how lovely." She dug her fork into the cake again.

I took a deep breath and continued. "I'd *really* like to go . . . and the only way I could, is if you—"

She put her fork down with a clang, and looked at me hard.

". . . if you come with me," I finished.

She tightened her lips. "You know I'm not keen on deceiving your parents, Jazz. Especially not now, when they've been so wonderful with all this madness. You know they're helping me with the legal bills, don't you?" She picked up the fork again.

I shook my head, my windless sails sagging.

"I'm sorry, Jazz. I will *not* deceive your parents."

And that was that.

When I got home, I did my homework, then dialed Mit. "I'm trying to get Auntie Kinder to come to New York and having zero luck. I need help."

"You do need help, but let's figure out the Auntie Kinder thing first."

"Ha, ha. Will you get serious, please?"

"I actually am. With Ken—whose real name is Josh, by the way."

"Really? You guys are getting serious?"

"Yep."

"Wow. Serious, like, if you were a straight couple you'd be talking marriage?"

"I'm in Canada, Jazzy—gay marriage is legal here, remember? We could totally talk marriage if we wanted to . . . but no. We're getting serious, as in like, maybe being exclusive."

"That's pretty serious."

"Yeah. And Tyler? Anything new on the horizon since you made out?"

For a moment, it felt like someone was playing giant drums in my belly. "No, nothing new."

"Hey, Jazzy, what are we gonna do about this party our parents want to have for us?"

"*Auf,*" I said. "It's SO annoying."

"Sometimes I really wish I could just come out to them and be done with it, you know?"

"*Do* I. It's a real pain, all this undercover crap. Even with Auntie Kinder—I mean, I *know* we're doing the right thing, I can feel it in my gut, but my parents would never go for it. It would be so much easier if they did and could help!"

"Speaking of which," he said, bringing us back on track, "Auntie Kinder. Getting her to NYC."

"Right. You have to help me, Mit. How do I get her to agree to going to New York?"

"How far is it from where you are?"

"About five hours. Why?"

"You said she looked like she needed a break, right?"

"Yeeeaaahhh. . . ."

I could almost hear him thinking. "You should tell her it'd be like a getaway. Tell her she needs to get away from all the crap she's been dealing with for just one night, and that she'll get to see a television show being shot. Oh—and tell her she'll get to be pampered in a hotel room—no cooking or dishes . . . you know—work it, Jazzy-style."

"Hmmm, you think she'll go for that?"

"It's worth a try."

I hung up with him and thought of ways to word convincing arguments for getting Auntie Kinder to New York City.

But something must've been in the cosmic air, because in the midst of planning Auntie Kinder and Dr. Babaloo's reunion, things were getting pretty heated in my own personal love life, too.

A couple of days after speaking with Mit, I was on my first "date" with Tyler. Okay, maybe it wasn't really a date, *per se.* He had asked if I wanted to "hang out" after school and I'd said yes without thinking. I didn't know how I was going to pull it off, but I knew I wasn't about to *not* go. This is what regular people did, without ever worrying about it. It's what Cindy and her sisters did all the time, and nothing horrible had happened to *them.*

I looked at the door of the restaurant as Tyler emerged with a large paper bag in one hand and a cardboard carrying tray with two sodas in the other. He handed both to me as he slid behind the wheel and put the car in gear.

It had been too easy to get my dad to agree to my going out. I took one of the cables out of the computer and told him it wasn't working. He came up, tried booting it up a few times, and confirmed that the thing was definitely broken. I gave him a panicked look and said that I had a really hard assignment due the next day, so could I please go to Cindy's to use her computer? And, *voilá. . . .*

"Mmm," I said, taking a deep whiff, "deep-fried carbs—my favorite."

He laughed. "I like a girl who likes to eat."

He said he liked me! Little fireflies fluttered all the way up my legs and into my belly. I busied myself with opening up the bag and rummaging through its contents.

I had told Cindy about the date because I had to, she was my alibi. But I didn't tell her that I had been late for just about every one of my classes that week on account of hanging out with Tyler at my locker, or dawdling with him in the halls.

"Careful," she'd warned. "You keep going like this and you're gonna be in over your head, Jazz."

As much as I didn't want to admit it, I couldn't help but wonder if my best friend was jealous. I didn't want to think about that right now, though. Especially since I was trying to remember how to breathe properly again.

I leaned out the window to look in the side-view mirror and checked the lipstick I'd borrowed from Mary that afternoon.

Tyler reached across to take my hand in his. His hand swallowed mine; it was cool and a bit rough, and my heart was at a full gallop. I couldn't turn to face him because I was so busy chewing my lip, but I laced my fingers through his.

Just when I worked up enough nerve to try to say something, we turned onto a small road leading to the lake. The road ended at the top of a hill that looked out over the whole town of Maple

Ridge. We were at Observation Point, and it was getting dark enough that the lights were beginning to slowly blink on.

"Wow, I've never seen Maple Ridge from here," I said after he turned the ignition off. "It's so pretty."

Tyler smiled. "Let's eat on the hood," he said, opening his door and taking the drink tray. He popped the trunk, pulled out a blanket, and spread it over the still-warm hood.

I jumped up onto it and began unwrapping my burger.

"You eating by yourself?" he asked, climbing up to sit next to me.

"Pardon me?"

"You can't wait thirty seconds until I get mine?"

"Oh! I'm sorry, I. . . ." I put down my burger and felt something singe inside my chest.

He looked at me steadily for a moment, then broke into a grin. "Just messing with you, Baby J." And then he leaned across to kiss me.

The uneasy feeling subsided, but I still felt a little off-center. Like I was walking on the balance beam in phys. ed. I ate only half of my burger, not feeling nearly as hungry as I was when we got here.

"What's the matter?" he asked, throwing his wrapper in the bag and reaching for his soda. "You're not eating."

I shook my head. "Nothing."

"Sure?" He cupped the back of my head, moving his fingers down to caress the back of my neck.

I put my half-eaten burger in the bag and smiled, shoving all weird doubts firmly aside. "Definitely."

He gave me this smile that made me want to climb into him somehow, and scooched up behind me. He pulled me back so that I was leaning against his chest, between his legs, and wrapped his arms around me.

I decided, right then and there, that I would do anything—anything at all—to have what I was feeling right this moment, as a permanent part of my life. How could a person marry someone not knowing if they'd ever feel like this in their arms, on the hood of a car?

So many kids in the world got to do this without hiding it. Without being afraid that someone would immediately force them into a marriage they didn't want if they ever got caught.

I *liked* this feeling. It was huge like the sky above us, and I wanted to follow it to see where it led.

We sat together, watching the lights come on across the lake. The sun hadn't gone down yet, but it was slipping slowly over the horizon. I knew I should get home soon, or at least call my parents. I remembered what Tyler had said before, and repeated it now. "Did you know that the ancient Indians—your people—used to say that when one sun sets, a thousand take its place?"

I felt his arms tighten around me. I dropped my head back against his shoulder and stared up into the sky. This time I knew what he was talking about. The stars, they were like a thousand suns. And at night, that's what they felt like, little pricks prodding everyone to do what's deep down inside, and not worry about anyone or anything else. They were like a veil, letting the secret part of you be heard—the part you kept shut and quiet under the harsher light of the daytime sun.

He pressed his cheek against mine. I could feel his smile.

My heart went slip-sliding into my stomach as he turned me around in his arms to press his lips against mine.

We kissed the same way we had on the bench in the parkette. Sweet and slow and soft. After a long moment, he slowly began probing with his tongue. Small, darting movements, then longer explorations. His hands crawled up under my shirt and found the front clasp of my bra.

I totally froze. He must have sensed it because he moved his hand away and, instead, he lowered me down until he was hovering above me. He continued to kiss me; his hands staying on the outside of my clothes. But his fingers touched places that shot sensations through my whole body and I felt like I was shattering—but in a way I liked.

I vaguely noticed the stars blinking on like the lights of the city as the sky turned from pink to bruised purple to an easy gray-black. I fought to keep up with what was happening inside of me, outside of me, *everywhere.* It was a kind of delicious I'd never known before. There was this desperate thing that I wanted to tear out of—like I wanted to outrun my body and expand and grow and then shatter into a billion pinpricks of light.

I pulled him against me, opening my mouth and giving in to the spiraling sensation. I was suddenly glad his car was so big. If we'd been on the hood of my parents' Toyota Camry, we'd have rolled off by now.

And then I gasped when I was rudely jolted out of my haze by a buzzing cell phone. *My* cell phone. I fumbled for it, but Tyler grabbed my wrist.

"I have to answer," I mumbled against his mouth. "It might be my parents."

"So what?" he said, kissing the side of my neck. "Tell them you had it turned off."

I wrenched myself away. "No, I have to get this." I took a moment to steady my voice and breathing before answering.

It was Cindy. "Sorry, Jazz, but your mom called here three times and I'm running out of excuses."

"Crud," I said. "Okay, I'll call her. Thanks."

She giggled. "You okay? You sound a little, um, out of breath."

"Talk to you later," I said, snapping the phone shut.

Tyler pulled me back to resume where he had left off.

I pulled away again. *Not* easy. "I have to call my parents."

"Okay," he mumbled, not easing up.

"Seriously, Tyler, I'll be in deep dung if I don't call them and get home soon."

He sighed and rolled over onto his back.

I hopped off the hood of the car, adjusted my clothing, took some deep breaths, and moved a few steps away.

My mom answered. "Hi, Mom," I said.

She plunged straight in. "Why aren't you using Cindy's home phone?"

"Oh, I'm . . . I'm in her backyard, um, just looking up at the stars."

"Stars? You can't see stars from your own backyard?"

I sighed. "Mom, it's for our . . . astronomy class—I'm identifying constellations."

I heard a snicker behind me and shot Tyler a warning look before taking a couple more steps away from him and the car. All my mom needed now was to hear the voice of a guy in the background.

She paused for a moment and my pulse sped up. "So? When are you coming home? And why were you in the bathroom for so long?"

I dropped my head in relief. "Uh, I think I ate something bad at lunch."

Another pause. "Are you okay now? Did you drink some ginger ale? That helps, you know. When are you coming home?"

"Yes, I drank some ginger ale, and it helped. I'll head out in a few minutes. I, uh, have a couple more constellations to look for."

"Fine. Let me talk to Cindy's mother."

"Huh?" *Crap.*

"Cindy's mother. Let me speak with her, Jassy."

"Um. . . ." I fumbled through my brain for something, and said the first thing that popped into my head. "She's in the bathroom."

"Hm. Funny, she must have had the same thing you had at lunch. She was in the bathroom the last two times I called. Hand her the phone, Jassy."

"She's giving herself a bikini wax," I blurted out.

That shut my mother up. "Oh. Well, come home, then."

I hung up and climbed back onto the hood next to Tyler. "I have to get going."

"So I heard," he said, looking up at the sky. "Bikini wax, huh?"

I felt my face grow warm.

He laughed. "Are your parents that strict?"

I nodded. "They put the FBI, KGB, IRA, and CIA to shame when it comes to monitoring me."

He grinned and looked at the sky again. "How long have you been in the FSL program?"

"Since I was a kid."

"Do you like it?"

"I used to hate it when I was younger because we got made fun of all the time, but now it's not too bad. I don't know what I'd do without Cindy and Jeeves, though."

He turned toward me and I saw a shadow flit across his face, but he didn't say anything. For just a few seconds, it felt like there was something tightly coiled inside him, ready to come unsprung. But before I could think about it, he jumped off the car.

"Come on," he said, "let's go." He put the blanket in the trunk of the car and came around to my side. His car was an old one with manual locks and windows. He unlocked my door and circled around the back to his.

As I buckled myself in, I thought of how nice it felt to have your door opened for you. Very Enrique-esque.

He turned on the radio and bobbed his head to the kind of hip-hop that Toni hates for the ten-minute ride. I asked to be let out half a block away so that I could walk the rest of the way to my house. If my mom saw me drive up to the house with a guy, I was toast.

As I watched him speed away, I wondered why it felt like I'd pissed him off. The earlier feelings I'd had had dissipated completely during that short ride home. I pulled out *Love's Wayward Journey* from my bag. "Hey, Charlotte," I said, looking at the heroine on the cover. "What would you do if Enrique got seriously pissed with you? And you had no idea what you'd done?"

Her lips seemed to curve into a tiny smile. A smile that seemed to say: *Find a way, Jazz.*

I tucked the book back into its secret spot in my bag. Maybe I was making it up? Maybe Tyler wasn't even upset. Maybe he had been focused on getting me home because he didn't want me to get in trouble.

Whatever it was, I knew this evening had torn a small opening into an area of life my parents had never wanted me to see. I got a glimpse of something that felt unbelievable. Something that made me feel a part of the world I was so separate from—the world in those hip-hop videos, the world Cindy and her sisters lived in. It felt exciting and free. And I wasn't about to let it go without a fight.

Chapter 14

Things were getting worse for Auntie Kinder. Another letter arrived, certified mail, from her ex-husband's lawyer. And the weekend Mary had booked the studio and equipment was coming up fast. I couldn't talk to Auntie Kinder Thursday while I hung out with Pammi, so I went over on Friday. I told my parents I was just going for a bit and headed over. I was eager to try out Mit's suggestion. If I couldn't get Auntie Kinder to agree to go, the whole Plan would be a bust.

A part of me wished I could talk to Auntie Kinder about Tyler like she and I used to talk about boys and crushes. But something fundamental seemed to have changed. Her life was so much heavier now and my love life seemed so . . . I don't know, *small* in comparison.

"Auntie Kinder?" I said when Pammi left the room. "I'm going to ask you something and would like you to just hear me out, okay?"

She was laying on the sofa with the remote in one hand and a lemonade in the other. She cocked her head to one side and looked at me. "Go on, then."

"Okay. You know I want to go to New York."

She gave me one of her looks.

"Wait. Just hear me out, please?"

She gave me another look, but nodded.

"I think it would be good for you to go, too. Just go and get away for one night—spend the weekend with the girls. All of us; Pammi, too. We could get away from everything—rest, no cooking, no dishes— then come back to face everything again."

She was quiet for a moment. "It is tempting, I'll give you that."

"Come on," I urged. "It'll be fun! And you can come back feeling a little more rejuvenated."

She dropped her head back and rubbed her forehead. "I simply can't afford it right now, Jazz. Your parents have been lovely throughout all this legal business, but it's still a strain on me and Pammi."

"We'll all pitch in! There will be so many of us that it'll be totally affordable. Come on. . . . Think of it—one night in a hotel room in New York City, away from all this crap." I waved at the piles of papers and documents on the table.

I meant what I said. Mary and Toni had already said they would cover most of the expenses—they could write a lot of the trip off as a business expense if they visited some of the trade wholesalers while they were in the city.

"I really don't know, Jazz. . . ."

"And you wouldn't have to deceive my parents," I added. "It's all legit."

She looked over and gave me a weak smile. "It does sound good."

"So you'll do it?" I held my breath. If Auntie Kinder had felt something like what I felt when I was with Tyler when she was with Dr. Babaloo, I couldn't imagine what it must've done to her to be ripped away from that and forced to marry the giant A-hole her parents had found for her. And now she was still suffering over it—she really did need a break.

"Let me think about it."

I clapped my hands together. "That's perfect! Take all the time you need."

"What'll you girls do there? Shopping? Sightseeing?"

I nodded. "Yes." Hope blew into me, expanding me like a balloon. "Some of that, for sure," I said. "But also, um, Cindy's sister, Mary, is shooting a TV segment for the local station that broadcasts from her college campus."

Auntie Kinder raised her eyebrows. "A TV show? Tell me more."

"It's a show about . . . about, um, I'm not exactly sure, but they're interviewing some celebrity."

"A celebrity?" She seemed to perk up a little.

I tried to leverage the interest in celebrity-ness. "It would be an educational experience for Pammi as well."

She sat silently for a long moment, during which a bead of sweat slowly made its descent along the peaks and valleys of my ribcage. Finally, she cocked her head to one side and gave me a stronger smile.

"Let me think about it," she said again. This time, her voice was clearly more positive and interested.

I think I heard angels singing.

The next day, I called to find out if she'd thought about it. She said she hadn't had a chance, yet. In fact, she didn't get a chance all the next day, either, because another letter came in the mail and threw her completely off balance.

Then on Sunday night, before the weekend Mary had studio time scheduled, Auntie Kinder ran the New York trip by my mom and dad after I'd been there talking it up with her again. They said it was a "wonderful" idea for Auntie Kinder and Pammi to get away for a bit. And that of course "Jassy should go to help out with Pammi."

I couldn't believe my parents agreed to me doing an overnight trip in New York City, though of course, I'd be with Auntie Kinder. And with the drive being over five hours each way, there was no way to make it a day trip.

"Oh—Jassy," my mother said, catching me on my way upstairs the next afternoon. "I've let Gurmit's parents know, just to keep them informed, and to assure then that you will be fully supervised. It would be nice of you to call Gurmit while you're away to show them you are a good girl, with strong character. And

Kinder and Pammi really need to get away from everything. It'll do them good."

I called Cindy on her cell. She was in the car with Toni and Mary, on her way to meet Wes. I could feel the excitement zinging through the ether-wires as they all shouted, "ROADTRIP!!"

When I told Jeeves about The Plan later that night, he told his mom he was joining our "educational excursion." He said he would just jump on a train to meet us since our rental van had no space left. I shook my head at the *blatantly* obvious double standard: there's no way on God's green earth that I could have "jumped" on a train to New York City.

All next week at school, during lunch, I hashed the plan out with Jeeves and Cindy. "It's pretty simple: we'll conduct an interview with Dr. Babaloo, so that Roger has something he can air, then bring Auntie Kinder in, preferably without Pammi."

Cindy blew a bubble with her fruity-smelling gum. "Why?"

"We don't know how Pammi will respond," I said. "She had this psycho for a dad, and she has no relationship with him now—who knows how she'll feel about a new guy entering her mom's life?"

"Good point," Cindy agreed.

"He's not a new guy to her mom," Jeeves said.

"Exactly," I said. "They can all figure out the details of everything after Auntie Kinder and Dr. B. meet."

"So how will we get Pammi out of the scenario?" Cindy asked.

I looked at Jeeves. "Well, that's where you come in, Cool J."
He raised an eyebrow in confusion. "Pammi has always had a bit
of a crush on you, dude."

Cindy grinned. "Aww, how cute!"

Jeeves scowled.

"So, I thought that you could be the one to keep her away
from the studio."

"Oh you did, did you?" His scowl quickly morphed into
annoyance.

I sighed. "Dude, be a team player, okay? This is not the time
to bring your individual concerns around. Keep your eye on the
mission."

Cindy smacked his arm. "Yeah, Jeeves. Be a team player."

His eyes could've sliced me in half.

"Anyway, Auntie Kinder and Dr. B. will discover how deeply
in love they still are with one another, they will sit down and give
Roger a great interview together, then Dr. B. will easily win
Pammi over, and they would all live happily ever after."

Cindy stared at me. "*That* is the plan?"

"Do you have a better one?"

She blew another bubble as she mulled it over. Then she
slumped into her seat. "Nope. I got nothing."

Jeeves continued to scowl, but said nothing.

We headed down to New York City that Saturday, after things
slowed down at Redalicious.

"Go ahead, girls," Ms. Reda said, waving them off. She looked like the blonde lady from the *Sex and the City* movies. "I've got it from here. Everyone who was going to get anything done has already been here. I'll be fine. Go and have fun!"

Did I mention that Ms. Reda was brimming with awesomeness? Not only did she raise three girls (and not just *any* three girls—the inimitable Reda-Rodriguez girls) on her own after her husband left her for their nanny, but she also ran a salon and was full of just . . . awesomeness.

On the way down in the rental van, Cindy, Mary, Toni, and I had been super careful not to say anything that might "out" our plan in any way. This resulted in a lot of suspicious questions from Auntie Kinder, interrupted only by Pammi's excited chatter.

"So, Mary, what's this television show about, then?"

I could see Mary shifting in her seat next to Auntie Kinder, who was driving. "I'm not exactly sure, myself," she said, giving a nervous laugh. "It's the brainchild of the producer's son, Roger Minh."

Phew. Good save, Mare.

But Auntie Kinder wasn't done, yet. "It's an interview, right? Who's the celebrity?"

Mary cleared her throat. "Well, I, uh. . . ."

Cindy jumped in. "I think it's a foreign celebrity, right, Mare? No one we would've heard of here."

I gave Cindy a covert thumbs-up. We braced ourselves for the next question, but luckily, Pammi began chattering about which celebrities she would *love* to see in person and which ones didn't "deserve a flashlight, never mind a spotlight."

There were a few more questions that Cindy and I were forced to field on our own, as Mary and Toni suddenly fell into a deep, coma-like sleep for the remainder of the ride.

When we finally got to the hotel, we had been in the car for way over the five or six hours it was supposed to take us. Clearly, the GPS did not take traffic and construction delays into consideration.

Cindy and I were in the room adjoining Auntie Kinder and Pammi's; Mary and Toni were next door; and Jeeves was across the hall. As I unpacked, I called my mom to let her know we had arrived safe and sound.

She had to have been sitting right next to the phone; it never made it through the first ring. "Oh, Jassy—*Rab da shukar*, you made it there safely! I was *so* worried. New York City is a very big place, *beta*. Stay close to your Auntie Kinder, *heh-na*? Call me after the show, I want to know everything, *accha*?"

I sighed. "Yes, Mom."

After we were all settled, Auntie Kinder and Pammi went out to do some exploring, and Cindy and I went to Mary and Toni's room. That was, by default, Plan Headquarters, since mine and Cindy's room was too close to Auntie Kinder's. Besides, Toni was the one who had made all the arrangements with Dr. Babaloo's "people"; she was a natural with all the business dealings she did on a daily basis at the salon.

"He's staying at the Four Seasons and has a driver dropping him off first thing in the morning tomorrow," she said as Mary let us in.

"I am *so* nervous," Cindy said, putting a hand to her stomach. "I have serious butterflies."

I was beginning to feel a bit queasy, myself.

There was a knock on the door. We all froze and looked at one another until we heard Jeeves's voice.

"It's me."

We heaved a collective sigh.

"Door's open," Mary called.

"So what's goin' on?" he said, gliding in to the room. He plopped down on the bed next to where I was perched.

I scooted over so he had more room. "Dr. Babaloo is getting dropped off first thing tomorrow morning."

Mary took a sip of her soda. "Roger will already be there," she said. "He works, like, twenty hours a day or something. He got a small crew to do the lights, cameras, makeup and all that. He's pretty psyched about this story."

Jeeves nodded. "It's a cool story."

Toni looked at her checklist. "Jeeves, did you bring your mom's DVDs of Dr. Babaloo's show? We need to give them to Roger tonight so he can watch them before the shoot."

"Got 'em," he said, pulling out his iPod. "Downloaded them before I left."

"Good," she said, checking it off. "Roger also asked us to come up with a list of questions that might lead 'organically' to an introduction to Auntie Kinder."

Everyone turned to look at me. I took a deep breath and considered that for a moment. "Hmm. I guess we should start with questions about his current work—how he got into it, what he focuses on, that sort of thing—then move on to his younger years and the people he was closest to. . . . You know, people who were instrumental in where he ultimately ended up, right?"

"And then we could bring in one of those 'instrumental' people," Cindy said, her eyes wide with excitement.

"Good idea," Toni said, writing quickly.

"Who's going to bring Auntie Kinder into the studio?" Jeeves asked.

"Why don't you?" Mary said. "You'll be with Pammi, anyway, right?"

"Yeah, but I thought the objective was to keep Pammi *away* from the studio."

Mary scrunched up her mouth. "Right. It would be nice for Auntie Kinder to experience the moment without worrying about anything."

"I don't think that's going to work," I said. "Auntie Kinder said she wants Pammi there because it'll be an educational experience for her."

"That's true," Cindy agreed. "Plus, did you see how excited Pammi is about it?"

We all pondered that for a moment.

Mary sat down on the edge of a chair. "How about if we give Auntie Kinder and Dr. Babaloo enough time to meet and get over the shock of it all, then bring Pammi in afterward, for the second part of the interview?"

"That might work," Toni said. "But how do we get Auntie Kinder to be okay with that?"

"Maybe," I said, looking meaningfully at Jeeves, "if Jeeves could find something that Pammi would just *love* to do New York City, instead of spending the entire day in a dark studio with grown-ups, Pammi will do that *for* us."

He looked at me incredulously. "Like what? How am I supposed to know what an eleven-year-old girl would 'love' to do?"

Cindy grinned. "Think about us in sixth grade. What did me and Jazz do all the time?"

He sat up. "No way. I am *not* taking her to a Courtney Pierce concert."

Toni laughed. "C'mon. Teen mags all say she's the 'pop princess of the millennium.' You'll probably have more fun than Pammi."

Jeeves shook his head vehemently. "No. Way."

"Hey," I said, suddenly remembering what Pammi had said the other day. "Doesn't the new Scary Daughter movie come out this weekend?"

Cindy jumped up. "Oh, yeah! I actually want to see that, myself. I saw the first three and they had awesome special effects."

Jeeves slowly nodded his head. "Okay, a paranormal thriller . . . Now *that*, I could get with."

I shook my head. Only Jeeves would say, "paranormal."

"Make sure you take her to the show that doesn't let out until *after* the interview," Mary reminded him.

"Gotcha, boss," Jeeves said, pointing at her, then heading for the door. "I gotta use the facilities."

"You can use our bathroom," Mary said.

He grinned. "You're gonna wish you hadn't said that, so I'll spare you."

Cindy wrinkled her nose. "Oh, gross! Yes, please—drop a bomb in your *own* bathroom."

"I've scheduled a pampering treatment for Auntie Kinder at a friend's spa for the morning," Toni said, scribbling in her book again. "One, Auntie Kinder needs some pampering, and two, we need her out of the way until it's time for her come in." She turned to me. "Jazz, just assure her that Pammi will be fine. Tell her that she's in good hands with us, and that Jeeves is a responsible, mature, stellar babysitter. Besides, the movie theater is only a few blocks away."

I looked at her in awe. "Wow, Toni, you've thought of *everything*. I'm sure Auntie Kinder would love some pampering at a spa!"

Mary gave her big sister a squeeze-y hug around the shoulders. "That's why Mom has her running the salon. She thinks of everything."

"I can't help my natural urge to be a controlling beyotch. Lucky for me, sometimes it works to my advantage." Toni said with a quick grin. "Anyway. Back to business. Let's start on the questions."

We came up with what I thought were some great questions that led logically and "organically" to a meeting with Auntie Kinder. When we finished, Mary and Toni took the DVDs to Roger at the studio and Cindy and I headed back to our room.

Once in the room, Cindy ripped off her shirt and announced, "I need a shower. I think there are fumes coming off my body."

I giggled and grabbed the remote. "I didn't want to say anything."

I flipped through the channels. Maybe watching "So You Think You Can Dance?" reruns would help take my mind off what was to come—and thinking about Tyler.

I had just plopped on the bed when there was a knock on the door, followed by Jeeves's voice. "Hey, open up, it's me."

I dragged myself up to open the door, then leapt back onto my spot in front of the TV.

Jeeves stretched out next to me. "Where's Cin?"

"In the shower." I turned and gave him a look. "Gawd, Jeeves—there's, like, a whole other *bed* over there." I shuffled over to make room.

He smiled and looked away. "It's not as comfy as this one."

I rolled my eyes and flipped through some more channels, wondering why I suddenly hyperaware of Jeeves's presence next to me.

"Hey," he said, sitting up so that he was next to me.

I kept punching the "channel up" button. "Yeah?"

"Check this out."

I turned around and my face collided with one of the mushy hotel pillows. "Hey!"

He laughed and pointed a finger. "You should've seen your face!"

I grabbed the pillow and whacked at him as hard as I could. I didn't get him as good as he got me, but I still cuffed him on the side of his head. "Hah!"

"That's it," he said, jumping up and grabbing another pillow. "It's on, Dhatt."

And we went at it. We each got some good whacks in, with a few real smacks here and there.

"Ow!" I yelled, when his hand made contact with my shoulder.

"What'sa matter, Dhatt? Can't take it, but you can dish it out? Huh?" He swung again with the pillow, getting me smack across one unprotected side as I rubbed my shoulder.

I teetered off balance and fell on the bed as he followed with a flurry of lighter whacks all over. "Cut it out," I gasped between a fit of giggles, as the pillow-whacking gave way to a tickle-fest.

I grabbed for his hands to push them out of the way, but he was too fast. He poked under my arms and against my ribs until I was doubled over from laughing so hard.

Then he collapsed next to me and we both lay still, breathing hard.

Jeeves turned on his side so that he faced me and propped himself up on an elbow. He was *really* close.

"Hey, Jazz. . . ." He paused, then started again. "I was wondering if . . . maybe, one of these days, you and I could, you know, hang out."

I suddenly needed a drink of water. "Hang out?"

He nodded and looked away. "Yeah, you know. Like, for real. Me and you, we could, maybe, hang out somewhere . . . together."

Was he *hitting* on me? Did he mean "hang out" as in study together? Or, like, *go-to-the-movies-and-make-out* hanging out? Instead of asking him, I repeated, "Hang out?"

He nodded, inhaling deeply.

"Um . . . I don't know, Jeeves. You know my parents. . . ."

At that moment, Cindy walked out in a towel. I jumped up from the bed and almost hugged her.

"Oh, hey, Jeeves!" She said, running back into the bathroom. She poked her head out to give me a *why-didn't-you-warn-me?* glare, when she suddenly stopped, looked from him to me and back, then lingered on the tousled bedcovers. "Uh, am I interrupting something?"

"No!" I said. "We were just, um. . . ."

She raised her eyebrows, with the tiniest hint of a smile on her lips.

Jeeves got up to leave and, without making eye contact, said, "Like I said, let me know if you ever want to get together to work on that calculus homework, Jazz."

I almost fell back in relief. "Definitely!"

Cindy buzzed out as the door clicked shut behind him. "What was *that* all about?"

I shrugged. "Nothing."

She sat down on the other bed. "Right," she said, squeezing some lotion onto her legs and rubbing it in. "He's totally crushed out on you, Jazz."

"He's not crushed out on me," I said, gathering my stuff together so I could get into the shower. "We're *friends*, okay?"

"What. Ever."

I paused before closing the bathroom door. "It's not like that, Cin."

She rolled her eyes and squeezed out some more lotion. "Yeah. I said okay."

I shut the door and blasted the hot water. Cindy didn't know what she was talking about. Me and *Jeeves*? We were too much like family. No way.

Besides, he couldn't possibly see me in the same way that he saw the hoochies he hung with at school. But then, how come I felt those . . . flutterings? They weren't like the frenzied, insane commotion inside when Tyler came around, but they were something. Maybe Cindy was right, and I just didn't want to see it. I totally didn't need something more to worry about right now, and Jeeves was my friend and I didn't want to have to negotiate him crushing out on me.

Doing my best to ignore the knots in my stomach, I refocused on The Plan. I hoped it would go smoothly. I hoped Auntie Kinder and Dr. Babaloo could rekindle whatever they had all those years ago. I hoped Pammi would be okay. Most of all, I hoped I could get to sleep that night.

We couldn't, of course, sleep at *all*. If I was alone, I'd have been tossing and turning all night, and probably having nightmares about the next day, like Dr. Babaloo showing up with his new fiancée, or Auntie Kinder announcing she'd never stopped loving her ex-husband. But with Cindy by my side, I was a complete basket case. One moment she talked about how awesome it was that this amazing love story was unfolding in front of our very eyes, and the next, she was coming up with disaster endings worse than mine.

Finally, when Cindy was soundly purring in the bed next to me, I padded softly into the bathroom. I dialed Tyler's cell. I lost my nerve as the other line began to ring and hung up before he answered. I thought about what Charlotte would advise.

"Should I call him, Charlotte?" I asked the darkness surrounding me. Yes, I felt like an ass talking to a romance-novel heroine, but who the heck else was I going to talk to?

I dialed again, but hung up. I knew how late it was, and felt awful for calling and hanging up, but I just couldn't seem to control my fingers. I sat quietly for another moment and felt the darkness in the bathroom urging me to dial again.

This time, there was a click as the line engaged.

I punched the *End* key and took a deep breath to steady myself. I dropped my head in my hands and squeezed my knuckles against my closed eyelids. I wasn't one to pray, but right then, I prayed to whoever was listening to please help me get through the next day.

Chapter 15

I wish I could say it all went off beautifully. I wish I could tell you that Auntie Kinder and Dr. Babaloo were nestled inside a cozy booth in some expensive New York City restaurant right at this very moment.

But what actually happened was this:

The next morning, Cindy and I said good-bye to Auntie Kinder and Pammi as Jeeves knocked on their door. Then, as we hurried to the television studio, which was only a couple of blocks from the hotel, I got a call from Mit on my cell.

Cindy and I were on our way to meet up with Mary, Toni, Roger, and his crew, but Mit's close-to-hysterical voice stopped me dead in my tracks.

"My parents caught me making out with Josh."

It took me a moment to figure just what, exactly, those words actually meant. And then to figure out what they meant to *me*. And then I couldn't breathe.

Cindy looked at me with alarm. "What?" she mouthed frantically.

"They . . . *what*?" I asked, when my voice finally came back.

He sniffled. "They were supposed to be gone for the weekend, but the flight was canceled due to bad weather, and instead of waiting at the airport they came back home, and Josh was here and we had the music on and we'd already had a couple of beers, Jazzy—I totally screwed up!"

My knees kind of buckled under me and I reached out to grab Cindy. "Oh . . . my. . . . What *happened*? What did they say?"

She steered me toward some steps outside a rowhouse and whispered, "What's going on?"

I turned to her. "Mit's parents caught him making out with his boyfriend."

Her jaw dropped and she said no more.

"We are so up the creek, Jazzy."

"We?"

"Are you kidding me? My parents wanted to put the marriage in, like, shotgun mode! They wanted us to get married, like, tomorrow! I told them you knew and that we had a deal—"

"Don't tell me. . . ."

". . . They called your parents."

My lungs collapsed.

"They told your parents this marriage couldn't move forward because they just couldn't have a daughter-in-law who spends nights on her own in big cities and cuts her hair to impress strange boys."

"What are they *talking* about?" The phone trembled against my ear. "Your mom said she liked my hair!"

"Well, she told your parents that she and my dad gave it some more thought and decided you're not fit to be married. They said they'd tell everyone in the community!" The last part was almost a howl.

"Wait—*what*? Why would they say that about me?"

"Don't you see?" he moaned. "If they ruin your reputation first, anything your parents say will come off as defensive name-calling. They'll look like they're making things up to cover their asses and yours!"

"But they're the ones making things up!" I screeched.

"I know," he said, sniffling again. "They just can't face it, Jazz."

"What did they . . . say to *you*?" I asked.

"They said I'm dead to them."

I shook my head. My arms were almost numb from gripping the phone so tight with one hand and holding on to the cement step beneath me with the other. "Where are you now?" I whispered.

"I'm at Josh's. His parents know, and they're letting me crash on their couch. They are so cool." I could hear the tears in his voice.

"Mit. . . ." I didn't know what to say again. "I'm so sorry," I said softly.

"It's okay," he managed. "I'm eighteen—it's time I got out on my own anyway, you know? I never even wanted to be a friggin' foot doctor!" He tried to laugh, but it came out sounding like a strangled cry.

I told him to take care of himself and promised to call once the crap hit the fan on my end.

When I hung up, I dropped my head in my hands.

Cindy put an arm around my shoulders and said, "Holy sheets."

"This is bad," I said numbly.

"What can we do?"

"My parents haven't even called me yet." I shook my head. "That means they're either on oxygen at the hospital or this is real, *real* bad."

"What should we do?" she asked again. "Should we call the studio and try to cancel this whole thing?"

I groaned. "There's no way to stop it now—The Plan is already in motion. Dr. Babaloo's probably on his way to the studio, if he's not there already!" I took a deep breath to steady myself. "My life is already a disaster, Cin. The only thing I can do now is keep it from becoming a *worse* disaster."

Famous last words.

I got up, brushed myself off, and Cindy and I speed-walked to the studio.

~ * ~

It was all so surreal, with a lit set, soundproofed quiet, and people running around with headsets and walkie-talkies. I vaguely noticed that Roger was indeed nice-looking, in an oldish kind of way, and that he was super nice, too.

He had watched the DVDs and wanted to talk to me and Cindy about what we knew about "The Dr. B. and Auntie K." story. Cindy and I clicked into autopilot and told him everything Auntie Kinder, my mom, and Pammi ever told us.

There were lattes for everyone and a table set up with donuts and muffins, and Cindy and I ate nervously, non-stop.

"*That*," Mary said, pointing to the table, "was my job last summer."

A couple of guys in headsets rushed to the front door, and everyone turned to watch as Dr. Babaloo walked into the studio.

My first thought was that he was a lot taller and thinner than I had expected. He had his trademark donut-Indi-fro thing going on with his head, and his smile was instantly recognizable.

Roger strode up to him and introduced himself. "Dr. Babaloo, so nice to finally meet you. I've seen your show and I'm definitely a fan."

"Nice to meet you, Roger," Dr. Babaloo said, taking Roger's hand and pumping it.

I noticed Dr. Babaloo had a deep, warm voice. The kind of voice that would patiently help a seventh grader through a tough math equation. I was beginning to feel just a teensy bit better.

Cindy, Mary, and Toni all rushed up to say hello and get a closer look. I hung back, terrified of being exposed as the culprit who wrote the letter that started all this. A letter that, at the time, was a complete lie. And since one lie just caught up with me about half an hour ago, I was worried there might be something in the air. I just wanted all of it to be over, but making sure this plan went off without a hitch was of the utmost importance right now.

The guy doing Dr. Babaloo's makeup had jet black hair that flopped over one eye like a puppy's ear. His teeth were yellowy-brown and stacked up in front and behind one another, and his face was seriously pock-marked. But Dr. Babaloo looked fresh and camera-ready, without a hint of shine anywhere, when he was done.

The interviewer, an old guy with a graying beard, did a great job of making the whole interview seem as if it were in a comfortable living room. Dr. Babaloo laughed, shared openly, and winked a lot.

"He's amazing," Mary whispered next to me.

Cindy nodded on my other side. "He's perfect for Auntie Kinder."

Toni, who was sitting on a stool in front of us agreed. "I can see how the two of them would hit it off."

"They're soul mates," I said, automatically.

As the interviewer skillfully eased the questions into ones about Dr. Babaloo's childhood, a small ruckus turned everyone's attention to the front door.

In stormed an irrate Pammi. "Where's my mom? Where's Jazz?" she demanded, as her eyes adjusted to the lighting.

"Cut!" yelled the director.

Pammi saw me and stomped over just as the door opened again and Auntie Kinder came in, followed closely by Jeeves.

"What happened?" I asked, as Pammi came and stood next to me with a hand on her hip.

"Yes, what happened?" Auntie Kinder asked, shooting daggers at Jeeves.

"The movie was boring." Pammi said. "But he wouldn't let me leave the stupid theater!"

Jeeves looked at me. "She wanted to sneak into a different movie."

Pammi pouted. "My friends do it all the time! Why should I sit there and watch a crappy movie if it sucks?"

"The one you wanted to see was not appropriate for a sixth-grader!" he said, turning red.

"You're not my dad!" Pammi yelled back.

Auntie Kinder rubbed her temples. I was sure the effects of her spa treatment were quickly wearing off. She had an awesome manicure, though.

Just then, a deep, warm voice boomed, "Kinder?"

Auntie Kinder froze. All the color drained from her face as she turned, in liquid slow motion, to face the source of that voice. Her jaw dropped and her arms fell to her sides.

Dr. Babaloo took about three long steps and was in front of her. "My God, is that you, Kinder?"

Auntie Kinder inhaled, a deep ragged breath, and only shook her head, as if she couldn't believe what she was seeing.

No one moved. The entire studio stood still, holding its breath. Even those who didn't know what was going on could feel the tension in the extended pause before Pammi spoke.

"Who is this, Mom?"

Dr. Babaloo said tenderly, and without taking his eyes off Auntie Kinder, "Mom."

Auntie Kinder shook her head again, like she was coming out of a daze, and turned to face me. "JAZZ."

I had never before heard my name said with so much anger—no, *rage*. Numb as I might've been before, I turned to stone on the spot as everyone's eyes settled on me.

"Who's this guy?" Pammi asked again, more loudly this time.

Auntie Kinder, trembling and teary, grabbed Pammi's hand and strode right out the door without another word to anyone.

After the door shut behind her, the whole studio flew into chaos. Roger and Toni were looking at notes they had both written, people ran around, and there were shouts of "Lunch!" and "Take five!"

Cindy put an arm around my shoulder, saying, "Jazz, *breathe*." Mary ran after Auntie Kinder and Pammi. Jeeves shoved his hands deep into his pockets and walked out of the studio behind Mary.

Dr. Babaloo crossed his arms in front of his chest and turned to me. "So. Jazz, is it?"

I fled.

I didn't even answer Dr. Babaloo's question. I took off until I was back in the hotel room. By myself. I crawled under the covers and just lay there until I heard the sound of the front door to the adjoining room open; then, one by one, everyone's voices as they entered.

The door between my room and Auntie Kinder's was shut and locked, from their side. I could hear Cindy, Mary, Jeeves, and Toni talking to what sounded like an angry, hysterical Auntie Kinder and a very pissed-off, confused Pammi.

Without thinking, I reached for my cell phone and dialed Tyler's number. It had to be one of the dumbest things I'd done yet—and I admit there were many to choose from. I tried to keep my voice from sounding too hysterical, though I don't know if I completely managed to pull it off.

There was no answer, but this time I forced myself to leave a message. The voice mail cut me off before I finished my long, rambling, probably incoherent message, so I called back and left another one, just as long, rambling and incoherent as the first.

When I hung up, I smacked my forehead. What was wrong with me? I buried my cell phone under my socks in a drawer before I could make everything *way* worse by texting an apology to Tyler or something.

I grabbed *Love's Wayward Journey* and walked to the other side of the room. "Okay, Charlotte," I said, plunking down in an armchair. "You gotta help me out here. I am on the frickin' plank with a gun to my back and the violent Atlantic thrashing underneath me."

Silence.

I looked at her vulnerable, yet fierce face on the cover and bent down to put my head on my knees. I buried my face in my jeans as the pinpricks of tears started attacking my eyes.

Snippets of the conversation in the next room drifted to my ears. I heard Toni's calmer voice explaining things, Jeeves's occasional three-to-four word sentences, Cindy's soothing voice, and Mary's disappointed, yet wistful urging.

After a little while, Cindy poked her nose in. "You okay?"

I shook my head with my face still pressed against my knees.

Her eyebrows were knitted together in concern. "Come in," she whispered, waving me into the other room.

I looked up at her with an I'd-rather-shave-my-head-bald look.

She put a hand on her hip. "Get in here."

As soon as I walked into the room, I wanted to turn right around and lock myself back up, alone, in the other room.

Auntie Kinder stood up. "Jazz, I am very, *very* disappointed in you. How *dare* you meddle in my personal life! Do you have any idea what you have done—the kind of mess you have made? I should have paid attention to my inner voice when I was having doubts about this trip. . . . I should have known you were up to something!"

"Jazz didn't do it by herself," Jeeves said.

"For shame," she said angrily. "The whole lot of you, conspiring to turn my life upside down."

"Auntie Kinder, we've been trying to explain. We only wanted to help," Cindy pleaded. "Jazz wanted you to have another chance at love and to help you get rid of your ex-husband for good. . . ."

Auntie Kinder threw her arms up. "Did it ever occur to any of you that you could've been making a worse mess for me to contend with?" She glared at each of us in turn. "They could have a field day with this in court! I'm already being called an unfit mother!" Her eyes filled with tears.

I looked at Pammi. She stared accusingly at me like I should just hurry up and dive off the plank into the Atlantic, already. Her look said it all: *You have betrayed every last shred of trust I ever placed in you.*

Before I could get anything out, there was a loud knock at the door. "Well, open up, then," a voice said. It was Dr. Babaloo. "I know you're in there, I heard the lot of you talking all the way from the lift."

We all froze and looked at one another. Auntie Kinder looked stricken and Pammi looked like she was about to blow.

Jeeves was the first to un-freeze and let Dr. Babaloo in.

He walked straight past all of us as if were weren't even there, and sank to his knees in front of Auntie Kinder. "Kinder. . . . I can't believe it's really you."

She shook her head and stared at the hands she was wringing on her knees. "I'm so, *so* sorry, Bubs. I had no idea what they were all up to! I can assure you that, had I found out, I would never have allowed anyone to disturb your life like this. . . ."

Now it was his turn to shake his head. "Kinder, this is like a dream. Not a single day has passed that I haven't thought of you in some form or another. I'd heard through the grapevine that you were in the U.S., but nothing beyond that. I've always thought about getting in touch, but I didn't want to disrupt the life your parents wanted for you. But I've always wanted to reconnect with you. . . ." He looked around for Pammi. When he spotted her, his face brightened. "You and your family—your . . . husband, your children."

I heard a sharp intake of breath from Pammi, who had been watching, in silence, along with us.

Auntie Kinder finally looked at Dr. Babaloo, for the first time since rushing out of the studio. "There's no husband." She looked away for a moment, then whispered, "It's a long story, Bubs . . . so much has happened. You have no idea."

Dr. Babaloo reached for one of her hands and folded it between both of his.

Her face softened through the tears.

It was like a rainbow.

Chapter 16

Dr. Babaloo extended his stay in the city and planned to "sightsee the rest of New York." Auntie Kinder and Pammi took the train back upstate because neither of them wanted to be in the same vehicle as me and my "co-conspirators."

So on the ride back home in the rental van, Toni and Mary were up front, switching off on driving duties, Cindy and I were in the middle, and Jeeves reclined in the back, snoring for the first twenty-five minutes. At least until Toni shifted the music to blast out the rear speakers.

"Hey! What the f—!" he said, leaping up and slamming his head against the top of the van.

Toni grinned in the rear view mirror. "That was for screwing up The Plan, Sahota," she boomed, turning the music down and back to the front speakers.

"Dude," he said, laying back down. "There was nothing I could do unless I physically restrained her. And I *know* I would not be sitting here right now if I'd done that."

Toni hit the turn signal to change lanes and shook her head. "No, you'd be sitting here. You just might have a few broken bones."

"And missing teeth," Mary snorted. She checked out her reflection in the side mirror. "Hey, take the next exit, Toni—I want to get a latte," she said, pointing to the rest stop sign.

"Good idea," I said. "Can we also slow this ride down a bit? Or maybe a lot? Or better yet, could we turn back and drive to Guatemala?"

"Awww," Cindy said, petting my hair. "You still haven't heard from your parents, huh?"

I shook my head. "It is *so* over for me. You do my eulogy, okay?"

"What happened? I mean, besides the whole Auntie Kinder thing," Jeeves asked from the back.

Cindy answered. "Mit—the guy Jazz's parents set her up with?—his parents caught him making out with his boyfriend."

Toni took her foot off the gas as she stared at us in the rearview with her mouth gaping. "Are you *serious*?"

Several cars honked as they passed us, some hurling colorful words out their windows. Mary blew them kisses while Toni got back up to speed.

"But what does that have to do with you, Jazz?" Mary asked, looking back over her shoulder.

"In order to take the scrutiny off them and their son, his parents have cast aspersions on my reputation as a loose, hair-cutting, New York City-traveling, bad Indian girl of questionable repute. Completely unfit to be married."

Toni hooted. "You go, Jazz!"

"You don't get it, Toni," I said softly. "I am *so* screwed."

She glanced in the rearview as she took the exit for the rest stop. "Your parents wouldn't do anything . . . *drastic*, would they?"

I swallowed the fear that bloomed in my chest and shrugged.

We were all silent as Toni pulled into the parking lot.

Mary slipped her sunglasses on and shook out her hair. "I'm going to get some coffee. Anyone else coming?"

I shook my head. "I'm staying in the car. Can you get me a Frappuccino?"

"Sure. Jeeves?"

He shook his head. "No, thanks. I'll stay and keep you company, Jazz—if that's okay with you."

I shrugged. "Sure." Then I narrowed my eyes at Cindy, daring her to give me that look.

She grinned, but bounced away quietly.

Jeeves settled into the middle seat with me, where Cindy had been. Toni left the keys in the ignition, so we turned the music back on.

"Hey, Jazz, that's pretty serious—what Mit's family is doing."

"Yeah." I nodded and looked out the window on my side.

"Your parents are going to freak."

I nodded again, fighting back panic and tears. My voice was strained. "Thanks, Jeeves. No need to state the obvious, but thanks."

He reached out and mock-punched my shoulder. "Sorry."

We sat awkwardly for a moment as the opening beats of "I Kissed a Girl and I Liked It" began playing.

"Hey, Jazz," he said, leaning forward to turn the music down.

I turned to face him. "Yeah."

"You know, I would marry you if those guys ruined it for you forever."

I laughed. "That's sweet—a pity marriage!"

He shrugged, and I realized he must've meant what he said.

"We are *so not* ready to get married, Jeeves. Besides, even if our parents approved, my parents want me to marry someone way richer than we are." I was only half joking.

"I am gonna be way richer than we are," he said, grinning. But then quickly sobered. "If you ever wanna talk to someone," he said, "call me, okay?"

Suddenly, tears sprang to my eyes. There was a huge rush of things I wanted to say and all these feelings crammed into my chest, struggling to make it through my throat and out of my mouth.

Jeeves sat perched almost on the edge of the seat, waiting and listening intently.

I opened my mouth to tell him . . . well, I didn't know what. But to tell him *something*. Maybe that I was so glad he was there, right that minute. Maybe that I was glad he "got" it and got *me*. Or that him saying just those few little words talked me off a kind of ledge.

But then Mary opened the door. "Here's your Frappuccino, Jazz."

She shoved the drink toward me, then stopped abruptly and stared at each of our faces in turn. "Um, here, I'll just put your drink in this cup holder and I'll, uh, run to the ladies' room. Be right back!"

But it was too late. The moment had passed—at least for me. I suddenly became super self-conscious and sipped on my Frapuccino as Toni came back and climbed into the passenger seat, rambling on about how they messed up her order at Taco Bell.

When I got home, things were far worse than anything I could've anticipated. Auntie Kinder had told my mom about what happened in New York City. So, on top of the Mit lie, there was also the Auntie Kinder lie. And all the little lies that held those big ones in place.

I had not been allowed to unpack, wash, use the bathroom, or any other act that might allow me to be a little more comfortable. The word "punishment" was etched all over my parents' faces.

As soon as I walked in the door, they both pointed to the sofa. And, given the current of rage coursing through the house, I obediently set my butt into a comfortable groove in the exact spot indicated.

My mother quickly followed with, "*Hiyo Rubba*, all those hours working hard for other people so you can have opportunities, and *this* is what we get!"

I knew that anything I said at this point would only make matters worse, so I stayed as silent as I could. Maybe if I was quiet enough and didn't budge, they'd forget I was there. . . .

My dad turned sharply to face me. "Do you have any idea what this will do to our entire family?"

"Such deception!" my mother continued. They were a two-person firing squad. "Everything we've ever done has been for you, Jassy, from coming to this country, to the hours your father and I work and the sacrifices we've made! And this . . . *this* is how you repay us!"

"Mit's gay!" I blurted out.

The deathly silence that followed felt like February in my bones.

"*Enough* lies," my father said, his eyes pinning me to the spot.

"It's the truth! I *swear*. That's why they're making all that stuff up about me—"

"What *bakwaas!*" my mother yelled, shaking her head. "Do you believe this girl?"

"It's *true*," I cried. "He told me himself that first day we met at the coffee place!"

"*Bas*," my father boomed. "Indians are not gay!"

My mom turned to him. "There *was* that documentary we watched—you remember? From the British filmmaker . . . BBC special about the *hijras* in India and the gays."

My dad stroked his chin. "Ah, *han*. I do remember that now that you mention it."

"But regardless," my mom said, turning back to me.

"Yes," my dad agreed. "Regardless. We do not believe a word you say, Jassy. Your actions could destroy our family name for many generations to come. Your cousins will have their names attached to you and your—now soiled—reputation, and if their parents have a hard time marrying them off, *you'll* be to blame."

My mother nodded. "Our only choice now for a girl like you—"

"What's 'a girl like me' supposed to mean?" Boy, I just didn't know when to quit. It was as if the tongue-control guy in my brain was asleep at the dials. But when I got stung, I couldn't help reacting.

My mother thinned her lips, her eyes flashing like lightning bolts. "A girl like you—outspoken, feisty, irreverent, acting from your heart. . . ." Her eyes suddenly filled and she turned away.

My dad sighed. "Jassy, you must never deceive us again. Understand? This type of behavior will not be tolerated. You will finish up this school year, then you will go to India to live."

It felt like the floor dropped out from underneath me. I couldn't coax any words out of my throat.

My mom crossed her arms. "And as far as what you pulled in New York with Kinder—Jassy, you simply can't play with people's lives like that. Especially with matters of the heart . . . it's a very delicate and particularly volatile area."

She walked over to me, tilted my chin with her finger so that I was looking into her face. Her eyes were hard, but with a sadness in them that went way back into her depths. She spoke gently, even though her words hit me with the force of concrete blocks. "*Beta*, it's not good to get too caught up in the murmurs of the heart. They are deceptive, and could easily lead you astray."

And with that, I was released to my room. I felt as if I had a giant sack of boulders strapped to my back as I climbed the stairs.

In my bedroom, with the door shut, I turned to Charlotte. "She's wrong." My voice was a trembling whisper. "Auntie Kinder once said love is all there is in this life—that you have to find it, recognize it, and never let it go . . . even you, Charlotte, you left everything behind to be with Enrique."

After that, my descent was rapid. It was more of a freefall, really.

Chapter 17

I decided that if I was going to be shipped off to my country of origin, and had absolutely no more say in my future or my destiny, I would squeeze in the last little bit of whatever I could out of my (relative) freedom.

My parents didn't ground me like they did last time because, I guess, they figured they'd given me the grand poobah of punishments and that would suffice. Cindy and her sisters were stunned when I told them at Redalicious that following weekend.

"I can't believe they're actually doing it," Toni said, pouring hair-dye activator from a large jug into smaller, squeezable bottles. "I mean, I know you said they always threatened to, but I never really believed they'd actually do it!"

"I still don't think they're going to go through with it," Mary said from the waxing room. She was doing her legs.

Cindy folded a piece of foil paper onto the dyed section of Mrs. Middleton's hair. "Looks like they mean business this time, though."

"You're going out of business?" Mrs. Middleton yelled.

"No!" Cindy shouted. "Business is great, Mrs. Middleton!"

"Oh! Glad to hear it!" The old lady grinned her full set of big, fake teeth. Mrs. Middleton had been a happy Redalicious customer for something like a hundred years.

"So when do you go?" Toni asked.

"I don't know," I grumbled. "I have no details. No idea how long I'm going for, whether they plan to find me someone there to marry—nothing. Only that we leave after this school year."

"Oh, Jazz, that sucks large," Mary called out.

Mrs. Middleton turned around to Cindy and whispered loudly, "Did she say she's waxing balls?"

The next day, I ran into Tyler at the mall. I'd run into the Rite Aid to grab a box of tampons, and when I saw him, I kind of tossed them back on the shelf and scooted down to the toothpaste area.

"Hey!" I said, speaking loudly enough to be heard over the thudding in my ears.

He smiled. "Hey, Baby J.!"

I apologized profusely for calling from New York and leaving those humiliating messages on his voice mail.

He smiled. "I got your messages, but I didn't want to call back in case it got you in trouble with your parents."

I quickly summarized what we were doing there without adding the bit about Mit and our marriage scheme.

When I was done, he whistled. "Wow. *You* planned all that?"

I closed my eyes and shook my head. "I'm ashamed to admit that I did."

"I wouldn't be ashamed," he said.

The look in his eyes turned me into a puddle.

Just then, a little girl came running around the end of the aisle and threw her arms around his legs. "Ty! I couldn't find you!"

He swooped her up and held her in his arms. "I told you I was just going to the next aisle, buddy."

She pouted. "But then you didn't come back."

"I met a friend—Sianna, this is Jazz." He looked at me. "Sianna's my little sister."

I smiled into Sianna's night-black saucer eyes. "Hey, Sianna," I said. "I was looking at this Dora toothbrush. Do you think I should get it?"

She giggled. "You're too old for that."

I stared at her in mock disbelief. "Dude. I *so* am not. I *love* Dora."

She laughed. "You have a funny name."

I shrugged. "I've heard that before."

Tyler put her down and she ran down the aisle to look at the greeting cards. "You're good with kids," he said.

"I've been babysitting since I was about eleven."

He nodded, then looked over his shoulder. I looked to see what he was looking at, but he turned back around and planted a soft, warm kiss on my mouth.

Stole. My. Breath. Away.

"I gotta go, Jazz, but I'll see you at school tomorrow?"

I could only nod.

The next day, I met his family. I cut classes to hang out with Tyler, and after we spent over an hour making out at Observation Point, he said he needed to swing by his place to grab a few things.

When we walked in the door, he visibly tensed up. Both his parents were in the kitchen.

"Home early?" his father asked.

I stood motionless in the doorway, wishing I could disappear. I so knew what it was like to get caught, and I didn't want to make things worse for Tyler.

But, after the slightest hesitation, Tyler slipped off his shoes. "Study period."

"And you, young lady?" Tyler's father towered over everyone in the house. I noticed his salt-and-pepper moustache as he looked at me intently, his brow wrinkling together above his forehead. His accent was a little like Cindy's boyfriend's, but a bit more sing-songy.

I glanced at Tyler. "I, um, have a study period, too." I stammered.

"Your mother and I had a meeting with Sianna's pre-school," Mr. R. said. "Good thing; otherwise we'd never know when your study periods are . . . and who you bring home during the day."

Just then there was a movement behind Mr. R. A small cinnamon-skinned woman, with red highlights in her hair, stepped out and extended her hand. "I'm Kavita."

I shook her hand. "Nice to meet you. I'm Jazz."

She smiled warmly and covered my hand with her other one. "Welcome, Jazz. Please come in and sit down."

"Where your parents from, Jazz?" Mr. R. said, asking the same question his son had asked that first day we met.

I recalled what Tyler had told me about his father's views, and bit the inside of my cheek. "India."

"Huh," he said, narrowing his eyes just a little.

"Won't you sit down, Jazz?" Kavita asked, patting a spot next to her on the sofa.

I looked at Tyler as I lowered myself onto the sofa. He was leaning against the wall in the hallway where our shoes were. He still had his jacket on and his mouth had gone from the luscious lips I had just finished kissing, to a straight, thin line.

"Sit down, boy," Mr. R. said, pointing Tyler to the loveseat across from him.

Tyler didn't move. "We gotta get back to school, Dad."

"I thought this was a study period."

Tyler still didn't move.

Mr. R. turned to look at him. "I said, *sit down*, boy. All these hours I work so you could live in this big house and drive that big car." He swept his arms like he was showing off the palace grounds. "No respect, Kavita—these kids got no respect." His voice rose as he moved closer to Tyler. "How many times I gotta tell you things?"

Tyler kept his eyes trained on the window to their backyard as he walked to the loveseat. When he sat down, he stared at a spot on the tan rug.

"Jazz," Mrs. R. said. She smiled and leaned close like she was about to let me in on a secret. "I'm glad to see Tyler making friends at his new school."

I nodded, wishing I could beam both me and Tyler out of there.

"You Indians normally keep to yourselves, don't you?" Mr. R. said, getting up.

I darted a look from Tyler to his father. "I guess. . . ."

Tyler leveled his gaze at me, but I had a feeling he wasn't seeing me at all.

"When I was growing up, them Indians didn't like to mingle with us locals, you know." He made a face. "Think they too good for us."

I shifted uncomfortably in my seat.

"Was a girl there—an Indian girl—I wanted to marry. But her family would have none of it." He looked at me and curled his mouth into something like a smile.

Mrs. R. laughed nervously. "Wasn't because she was Indian she wanted nothing to do with you." She looked at me and winked. "Girl was smart."

Mr. R.'s jaw tightened. "I want your opinion, I'll ask," he said in a low voice.

Mrs. R. visibly shrank back.

Tyler looked at his father. "Dad, we gotta go. Jazz has to get home."

Mr. R. stood up and walked to their entertainment center. He picked up a CD and popped it into the player. "Don't worry," he said, "stay a few minutes more." He laughed as he looked from Tyler to me. "You came to have a good time? I don't see no books for your 'study period.'"

I clasped my hands tighter on my lap. I wanted to bolt, rewind back to the front seat of Tyler's car, or just disappear and pretend I never caught this glimpse into Tyler's private world. A world far, far removed from the plush, rich-boy world I'd first envisioned him in.

A slow, grinding Caribbean beat pulsed out of the speakers. Mr. R. started moving and swaying to the rhythm.

Tyler stood up. "We're leaving, Dad."

His father shoved him back down. "Sit down, boy."

Tyler sat down and dropped his head into his hands. And that's where it stayed until we left.

Mr. R. danced his way to me and held his hand out.

I looked at Mrs. R. She smiled, but in her eyes there was something else. Something that I was sure mirrored what was going on in my own eyes. I swallowed hard and took Mr. R.'s hand.

He pulled me close enough so that I got a good whiff of the alcohol on his breath. Then he danced me around the room for a few moments as he sang along with the music. One of his hands stayed low on my waist—practically on my butt—for way too long.

A million thoughts zipped around in my head like birds that had suddenly escaped their cages and were flapping around a small apartment. I caught glimpses of Mrs. R., twisting her fingers together on her lap, and Tyler with his head in his hands.

When the song ended, Mr. R. released me. "Thank you for the dance, Miss Jazz," he said with a bow. Then he laughed and looked at Tyler. "Come back soon, and we'll do it again!"

Tyler stood up, slipped on his shoes, and stormed out of the house. I followed quickly behind him, awkwardly waving good-bye to Mrs. R. as I slipped into my boots.

Mr. R.'s singing followed us down the hall.

I struggled to keep up with Tyler as he strode to where his car was parked.

When we reached the car, he stood for a moment, lost in thought. He was right next to me and miles away all at the same time. Then, before I knew what was happening, he grabbed my elbow, whirled me around and shoved me hard against the passenger door.

The air was literally knocked out of my lungs and I couldn't breathe for a second.

"Why did you let him do that to you?" he growled into my ear.

I gasped for air. "I . . . I. . . ."

"If you ever pull anything like that again, I swear, I'll. . . ." He gave me a shove before letting go.

I slid down against the car and crouched on the ground, wrapping my arms around my body. I stared at the ground. *What was happening?*

Tyler kicked the tires and paced and pounded on the hood.

A few minutes later, he sank to the ground next to me. "I'm sorry," he whispered.

"H-He's your dad, Tyler. . . ." I stammered. "I . . . I didn't know what to do."

He pulled me into his arms and kissed the top of my head. "I know. It's okay. I didn't mean to be like that."

After a while, he stood and helped me up. When we got in the car, he leaned across, cupped my chin and whispered, "Kiss me."

Nothing mattered after that. I wanted him to kiss me hard enough to blot out everything. His dad, my parents, Mit, Auntie Kinder, Pammi, Dr. Babaloo . . . all of it. I didn't want to think about anything. What my future might hold—and who might be in it.

Chapter 18

In the next few weeks, I cut several more classes and racked up a few more absences. And still, the principal, Mr. Steinke, still said, "Keep up the good work, Jazz-beer," whenever he saw me in the halls.

He made it a point to know who all the FSL kids were. Every year, at the beginning of the school year, he held a special assembly honoring the students who made Maple Ridge a "vibrant and proud community." Everyone in the FSL classes got called up to the front and had their picture taken for the newsletter.

Cindy had left me a voice mail message and texts, but I was too busy with Tyler to return them. Somewhere in the back of my mind, I knew I was letting things fall apart. But none of it seemed to matter.

Then on the second Saturday I was going to miss work, Toni asked, "What the hell's going on with you, girl?"

I had gone in to Redalicious to pick up my paycheck and tell them I wasn't going to work that day. I said I wasn't feeling well, but the truth, of course, was that I was going to spend the day with Tyler.

"What do you mean?" I asked.

"There's nothing wrong with her," Mary said, coming out from the back. "This is about a guy."

"Cindy told us about the guy you've been dumping everyone for," said Toni accusingly.

"I am *not* dumping anyone for him."

They didn't press it, but I knew the Reda-Rodriguez sisters weren't happy about my skipping work, among other things. I felt like crap walking out of there after lying to them, but it all seemed totally worth it when I thought about seeing Tyler again.

No one understood. My parents—forget it; Auntie Kinder was caught up in her own super-serious problems; Cin had a "normal" life with a cool mom and cooler sisters; Jeeves's parents were more understanding and, plus, he was a guy. Mit was the only one who came even close to understanding, but, like Auntie Kinder, he had his own problems.

To make matters worse, Pammi had completely shut me out after New York City. Today was the first Thursday since the trip— which was almost three weeks ago—that Auntie Kinder asked me to come by and hang out with her.

"Jazz," Auntie Kinder had said on the phone, "I may forgive you for going behind my back and meddling in my affairs, but I will never forget. You'll need to go above and beyond to make it up to me."

I almost collapsed in relief. "Auntie Kinder, I've missed you so much! And I'm soooo sorry! I really just wanted you to be happy and to get ex-loser—I mean, your-ex-husband, out of yours and Pammi's lives, and I'm so, *so* sorry it worked out the way it did."

"What do you mean?" she asked, all innocence.

"It was a complete disaster, right?"

"Well. . . ." she said, not sounding horribly upset.

Apparently, after the New York interview, Dr. Babaloo extended his stay even further and was now staying in a suite hotel nearby. Indefinitely. His driver brought him out to our humble suburb daily to spend time with Auntie Kinder, and gradually, in increments, with Pammi as well.

So when I arrived at Auntie Kinder's today, Dr. Babaloo answered the door in a pair of jeans and a T-shirt, and Auntie Kinder had sweatpants on.

They were dressed more like me and my friends than people my parents' ages. "Glamorous date planned?" I teased.

"Very funny," Auntie Kinder sing-songed. "We're off to Kundalini in The Park."

"That sounds nasty," I said, grossing out on the thought of the two of them Kundalini-ing, whatever that was.

"It's a yoga-in," Dr. Babaloo said. "People are getting together to protest the gentrification of their neighborhood—demanding healing and natural life flow."

I stared at Auntie Kinder. "Natural life flow?"

Auntie Kinder gave me a look of utter annoyance. "Oh, Jazz, open your mind. The world is changing! People want truth. They want equality and justice, and they know when they're being lied to."

"Excuse me, but have you seen Auntie Kinder?" I asked, looking around the apartment. "I swear she was here a minute ago."

She threw a cushion at me and I ducked.

Dr. Babaloo laughed. "This is the Kinder I remember." He turned to her with absolute adoration in his eyes. "I remember the shirt you used to wear all the time: *Tree-huggers Unite!*"

I groaned. "How clever." Though I had to admit they made a really cute couple. "Where's Pammi?"

"She's in her room," Auntie Kinder said, raising one eyebrow. "Avoiding you."

I dropped my shoulders and sighed. This was going to be a long couple of hours.

After Auntie Kinder and Dr. Babaloo left for their yoga-healing-flow date, I knocked on Pammi's door. "Hey, Pams, it's me. Open up."

No answer.

"Pams. . . . I know you hate me for what I did with Dr. Babaloo—"

She flung the door open and stared at me indignantly. "That's *not* why I hate you."

I stared at her. "But you do hate me?"

"I don't *hate* you, but *you* used that word."

I exhaled in relief. "So then why are you so mad at me?"

She shrugged and went to sit on the edge of her bed. "I just wish you had said something to me. You know, she is *my* mother. And having someone new in her life means me having someone new in *my* life."

I followed her and nodded, feeling like a complete dingo.

"It's like you didn't think about me, not even a little bit."

I gave her a look of utter dismay. "But I *totally* thought about you, Pams!"

She put her hands on her hips. I saw water pooling in her eyes. "How?" she said, her voice cracking. "How was all that in New York about *me*?"

"Oh, Pams." I shook my head and dropped onto her bed. "All I could think about was . . . your father coming and dragging you away from us. From your *mom*. I just wanted to do something to help."

I watched helplessly as small tears slid down her face. After another minute or so, she dropped her hands and almost tackled me in a hug.

"I'm so sorry, Pams," I said, stroking her back. "I never wanted to hurt you. You're totally right. I should've asked you."

"Yeah, but it's probably better you didn't," she said, leaning across me to yank out several tissues. "I would *not* have gone for it."

I shrugged. "See? Can't win." I held up a hand. "But I swear: from here on in, I, Jazz Dhatt, promise to always consult you if I ever develop any more crazy-ass plans involving your mom."

She laughed. "Deal."

When I went home, I called Mit. I'd received a few text messages from him saying that he was fine. But every time I called, it went straight through to his voice mail.

This time, he answered.

"Dude, I can't tell which way is up, anymore," I said.

He sighed. "I know. I'm not doing such a great job, myself."

I sat at my desk and doodled on a scratch pad. "I just wish there was a manual, you know?"

"I know."

"There's all this stuff we're *supposed* to do. . . ."

"Or people we're supposed to like."

"Or not like."

"Yeah—that more."

"But there's no backup plan in case we don't *want* to do those things."

"Or like those people."

"I totally don't know who the real Jazz Dhatt is anymore."

There was a pause on his end before he said, "Maybe there isn't just *one* Jazz Dhatt."

"Huh?"

"Well . . . all this mess has given me tons of time to think about what I really want. I mean, I thought about running back home and telling my parents I'll do whatever they want. Telling them I'll settle down with a nice Indian girl and have kids and make them proud. Because I want that, you know?"

"You want a nice Indian girl?"

"No, you hazmat. I want my parents to be proud of me."

I nodded. "Yeah." Then added, "Me, too."

"But when I play that scene out, I realize I just can't go through with it. I'm a whole bunch of things. Complex. I love my parents, but—and I know this sounds dweeby—I love *me*, too. I want to be with Josh. Maybe not forever, but I want to be with a guy. Someone I choose and someone I pick, making all my own mistakes and learning along the way. And that's not my parents' idea of the perfect son."

"I've been doing some very un-perfect-Indian-girl things lately, too," I admitted.

"Really? Spill it, Jazzy."

I stared at my reflection on the computer screen. "I've been hanging around Tyler a whole lot and, well . . . let's just say my parents wouldn't approve."

"It sucks that it has to come down to picking either yourself or your parents, doesn't it? I mean, why can't we just have both, already?" There was deep sadness in his voice.

It was contagious. I doodled silently. Neither of us said anything for a moment.

"Jazzy, I gotta run. I'm supposed to meet Josh in, like, three seconds on the other side of town."

"Okay, but . . . Mit?"

"Yeah?"

"Is Josh . . . you know, The One?"

He sighed. "I don't know. I'm just taking it one day at a time."

The next day, Cindy kidnapped me at lunch. "Girl, I am so sick and tired of your AWOL crap," she said, grabbing me by the arm and dragging me away from my locker.

I clicked the lock shut and stumbled after her.

"You are having lunch with me and Mare and Toni today, and *that. Is. Final.* Got it?"

I craned my neck to see if Tyler was anywhere nearby. I hadn't seen him for days, and he hadn't returned my phone calls or texts.

"He is *not* here," Cindy snapped angrily.

I sighed and fell in step alongside her. "Cin . . . I'm sorry I've been kinda MIA lately—"

"Listen," she said, once we were outside. She turned to me. "I get that you're really into Tyler R., okay? He's hot and all, but you have become a whole different person since you started hanging out with him."

"What do you mean?" I asked, feeling my face heat up.

"I mean, a guy is no reason to dump your friends, Jazz. When things don't work out with you two, who is going to help you through it?"

I stopped walking. My voice came out louder than I intended. "What do you mean, 'when things don't work out'? Are you hoping they won't? Cuz if you are, that would be so skuzzy, Cin."

We were facing each other on the sidewalk, about half a block from the school. She raised her voice to match mine. "Of *course* it's not going to work out, Jazz—wake up! He doesn't care about you. He goes out with anything in boobs, or hadn't you noticed?"

My breath was coming out in shallow puffs and I noticed a few of the FSL geeks in front of us slow down and turn to look. "You couldn't possibly understand," I said through gritted teeth.

"I'm your best friend, Jazz, and as your best friend, I need to tell you the truth. Tyler R. is using you. He tries to sleep with anything that seems even remotely female! Has he ever told you what he likes about you? Do you two do anything together *other* than make out? Has he ever talked about being your boyfriend, or—"

"You are *not* my best friend," I said.

She stopped abruptly and stared at me. My hands balled up into fists and, for a split second, I thought I might belt her. Instead, I said real quiet-like, "You are nowhere *close* to being a friend. You'll never understand—you could never know what it's like to be me."

Then I stalked away. Cindy didn't know squat.

Still, her words gnawed at me as I stomped back to school. I remembered when Jeeves told me I looked "awesome." Tyler hadn't even said that much. I shrugged. Maybe that just wasn't

Jazz in Love

Tyler's way. Maybe he wasn't the complimenting type. Some people were like that—my dad, for instance. You needed a crowbar and wrench to get a compliment out of him.

But the thought didn't quell Cindy's voice in my head. So I decided that next time I saw Tyler, I would just ask him straight out: *Tyler, what do you like about me?* Easy peasy.

I went back to school, stopped in at the cafeteria, and picked up some fries and a bagel. I still had another twenty minutes before class began, so I took my food and sat outside on the grass, near the basketball courts, and crammed the food into my mouth. Shoving carbs down helped the stinging feeling inside subside.

Once I stopped seething, I took out my Latin homework. I suddenly wondered if part of the reason I was an FSL "genius" was because homework took me away from everything I never wanted to deal with at home. It gave me peace and privacy and an excuse to be away from the ever-future-planning eyes of my parents.

Just as I was about to conjugate the verb *vigilare*, a shadow fell across my notebook and a sweaty Jeevan Sahota plopped down next to me.

"Hey, Jeeves," I said, squinting into the sun.

He looked at my notebook. "Vigilo, vigilavi, vigilatus."

I smiled. If nothing else, you could always count on Jeeves to be consistent. "Veni, vidi, vici to you, too."

204

He grinned and looked out onto the basketball court. "The guys are not bringin' it today." He cupped a hand around his mouth and shouted, "Lame-ass suckers!"

Several of the guys turned to give him the single finger salute.

He saluted back. "Glad you're keeping up with your work," he said, still looking out onto the court.

"Who are you, my dad?"

He looked away. "Whatever."

I sighed. "I'm sorry. I'm trying to keep up, but I'm still woefully behind."

He nodded. "How's Tyler?"

"Fine," I mumbled. My stomach roiled at the mention of Tyler's name.

Jeeves nodded again and sat next to me for another minute before standing up and brushing himself off. "You walking home after school?"

"No, my dad's swinging by in the Ferrari," I said, shading my eyes.

He smirked. "I don't have practice today; I'll walk with you."

I nodded and watched him jog back to join the other guys.

I finished my lunch and worked on conjugations until the bell rang. When I dusted myself off and started toward the door, a familiar figure caught my eye. I turned to see Tyler. He was talking to a pale blonde from what Cindy and I sometimes referred to as the Bubblicious Boob Band. The sad thing was that most of those Triple Bs were really smart, and actually super nice.

I'd had conversations with a few of them and, once they were out of the vicinity of all manner of male-ness, they had no problems talking about college and real stuff. Once, I even had a conversation with a Triple B about MacBeth. But get them around a guy and they were all giggles and boobs again.

This Bubblicious was leaning against the brick wall and gazing up into his eyes as he leaned in to say something. One of his hands was against the wall on one side of her head, the other twirled a lock of hair around his finger.

My stomach clenched as I watched her giggle and thrust out her chest. Through a haze, I saw Jeeves walking toward the door from the other side. I straightened my spine and walked in.

My fingers were on autopilot as I opened my combination lock and pulled books out of the locker. I had no idea if I was pulling the right books. I just had to do something with my hands. Had to keep them busy so I wouldn't pound them against the wall.

Suddenly, Tyler was at my side. "Hey, Baby J.," he drawled.

Despite the queasiness in my belly, my legs felt like they would crumple. I looked at the floor, closed my eyes, and took a deep breath.

When I looked back at him, the commotion came back full throttle. "Who was that girl?" I blurted.

He stepped back. "What girl?"

"Outside. The blonde."

He leaned against the lockers and unwrapped a stick of gum. "Andrea?" he said, popping the gum into his mouth. "She's a friend." Then he looked down the hall. "Maybe like your friend Jeeves."

I slammed my locker closed and spun the dial on the lock. "Jeeves and I have known each other since we were in freaking kindergarten! How long have you known Bubblicious?"

He laughed. "You are so cute when you're pissed, Baby J."

And as much as I wanted to hate him . . . I just couldn't. Instead, I took all that anger and balled it up in my chest.

He stepped closer and cupped the back of my head with one hand, pulling me close. "She ain't nothin'," he said, right before his mouth found mine.

I melted against his chest, feeling that tight ball in my chest spread like a gas.

Two days later, I saw Tyler drive out of the parking lot with Wendy Johnson and her trillion-dollar extensions. His arm was around her shoulders as she snuggled against him.

Chapter 19

I got up each day after that, nearly threw up thinking about the possibility of seeing Tyler with yet another girl, then walked queasily to school, grinding my teeth the whole way. The absolutely *insane* thing was that part of me *wanted* to run into him.

I ached for the warmth of his hugs. I wanted to feel his breath against my ear. And I wanted *so* badly to hear him call me "Baby J." in that sexy, almost-lazy way that made me lose all feeling in my legs. Plus, not having Tyler there to take up massive amounts of real estate in my brain was dangerous. It left me lots of room to think about other things. Things like the fact that my best friend hated me, Jeeves was pissed because, among other things, I stood him up that afternoon we were supposed to walk home together, and the ever-looming trip back to my roots.

Mostly, though, I just didn't get it. I'd done everything right, hadn't I? I'd given up everything for love! I'd followed my heart! It was everything the books and movies told you to do! But then why did I feel like smushed doggy doo-doo?

The one good thing that came out of all this was that I was now making it to all my classes. Slowly, I was bringing myself back up to speed, and liking it. It felt good to remember who I was, to get back to stable ground—where I knew what to expect.

Before I knew it, May had snuck up and the trees had a haze of new green on their branches. All of Maple Ridge was buzzing over the upcoming, end-of-the-year dance. I thought about going, and up until the second week of not seeing Tyler, I didn't think I would. But after not seeing him for three whole weeks, I felt like I was suffocating in a hot metal box and clawing for oxygen. The stable thing was good for a while, but that pull to be close to someone (who's not your parents), to feel like they see and want this part of you that no one else can see—not your parents, your best friend, siblings, or *anyone* else. It's a special part of you that only someone who gets that close with you, in *that* way, can see— that was addictive in a way I could only find described, even remotely, in my torrid romance novels. Or, surprisingly enough, in romance flicks, both Bollywood and Hollywood.

One thing was becoming clear, though—I had to go to that dance. There was only one teeny-tiny problem, as usual: my parents.

The dance was in the evening and I wasn't talking to Cindy, so she clearly would not cover for me this time. That left me with only one possible alternative.

"Are you positively *mad*?" Auntie Kinder said when I asked her to cover for me. "After all you've put me through? You actually have the gall to ask me for something as outlandish as this? Your parents would have my head, for heaven's sake. Not to mention that if Pammi ever did something like this, I'd be devastated! No, Jazz, absolutely *not*."

Time to bring out some heavy artillery. "You *have* to help me. You're the only one who can. I, I've been . . . I was kind of, um, seeing someone. And . . . I think he might be my Dr. Babaloo."

She stopped wiping down the table and sat down in a chair next to me. "You *what*?" Her 'what' came out as *wot*. "Jazz, do you—do you think you might be in love with him?"

Bingo. "Well, I—"

Something flitted across her face. "Wait," she interrupted. "What's his name?"

I spoke immediately, without thinking. "Tyler."

Her lips thinned. "The same Tyler you've mentioned?"

I dropped my arms to my side in defeat. "Okay," I said, deciding to fess up. "I was seeing Tyler, and it didn't go too well. . . . I think I saw him making out with another girl—"

She stared at me. "You think you *what*?"

"Maybe it's nothing. Maybe they're just friends." That even sounded lame to *me*.

Her hand flew to her mouth. "Jazz!"

"Well. . . ."

Her face twisted in a jumble of incredible sadness and extreme outrage. "You sound like me when I was with my ex-husband. Making excuses!" She narrowed her eyes and brought her face closer to mine. "Promise me, Jazz, that you will stay away from this boy."

"I—"

"Promise me," she said without budging.

"Um, okay."

"Stay away from that dance, too," she ordered. "I mean that, Jazz."

It was clear I had to take matters into my own hands. I simply had to lie to my parents. No biggie. I was kind of used to it by now.

But by the time the dance rolled around, there was total chaos in the area behind my eyes, the area inside my ribcage, and the area behind my navel. I was a walking maraca, rattling all over the place.

When my dad left for work, I took a deep breath, walked into the kitchen and told my mom I had to go to a (made-up) friend's place to work on an assignment that was due the next week.

She inspected my face. "Can I trust you, Jassy?"

I nodded passionately. "It's important to me that you and Daddy trust me, Mom." Oh, man. I knew God was reserving a special place for me in that area set up for all the bad people. I couldn't believe what was coming out of my mouth.

She looked at me for another moment. "Okay," she said, letting out a long, drawn-out breath. "Go. Finish your assignment, then come straight home, *beta*."

When she said *beta*, the term of endearment she and my dad always used for me, but that I hadn't heard them use in *ages*, a thousand razorblades twisted, all at once, inside my stomach. I turned away before the lies showed up on my face, erupting like enormous zits to get me back for being such a crappy daughter.

"Remember to take your cell, Jassy."

"Okay," I managed, as I walked toward the staircase.

"And keep it turned on," she added sternly.

"Yep."

I tried to dress casually, so as not to arouse suspicion, but I took some accessories that I slipped on along the way. Trying to still the trembling of my hands, I slid on a shiny, deep burgundy lip gloss that I had picked up from the drugstore across the street, put some gel in my hair to smooth it down, and then ducked into the post-office bathroom to change into a mini-miniskirt.

When I arrived at the school, there was hardly anyone there. So when Madame Peltier, the French teacher, asked me to help set up the snack table in the hallway, I was happy to have something to do. I even agreed to staff the table until the actual snack attendant showed up.

The DJ was already set up and playing tunes, even though there were, maybe, three people in the gym. But the music was pretty good. I went outside a couple of times to call my mom with fake updates on my progress with my assignment.

When I was inside, every time the doors opened and more people walked through, my hands started shaking. I imagined how I'd avoid Cindy when she walked in.

But by the time ten o'clock hit, Cindy hadn't walked through the doors and neither had Tyler. I looked around. In fact, it seemed that no one I knew was at this dance at all.

I was at a dance that I had lied to come to—that I had promised Auntie Kinder I *wouldn't* come to—on the off chance that I might see a guy who clearly had moved on in the dry-humping chain. My best friend was not here. My parents didn't trust me. And they shouldn't. I was completely untrustworthy. I was a horrible best friend. I was easily replaceable.

Suddenly, it all came crashing down around me and I began to get a collapsing feeling in my belly. I grabbed my bag and went to the bathroom. I looked underneath the doors to make sure no one else was in there before I did something like freak out or cry or hurl. Luckily, no one else was in there. I went into the stall in the far corner and slammed the door shut just as the door to the bathroom opened again, letting in a burst of music.

I took several gulps of air to calm myself. Outside the stall, I could hear two girls giggling. I peeked through the crack between the door and the frame and saw that one of them was Bubblicious, the same one that Tyler had been talking to against the wall that day. Lovely.

She was with a carbon copy of herself, but with jet black hair. Together, they looked like older versions of the Bratz dolls that Pammi used to play with when she was little.

I sat on my heels on the toilet seat and tried to keep as still and quiet as possible.

"It was, like, *so* hot," Bubblicious said.

"Wow, that's awesome!" her sidekick bubbled.

I rolled my eyes and wiped the lip gloss off my mouth. This conversation wasn't even worth eavesdropping on.

Bubblicious lowered her voice. "We totally did it. At Observation Point. He says he likes the way I say his name, so I say, '*Tyler*,' all the time and he does this thing, like, when he wants to kiss me? He, like, pulls me close and whispers, 'Kiss me.'"

Sidekick squealed.

I put my palms against the wall to either side of me. The underwire on my bra grew damp as I tried to calm the trembling of my legs. I really didn't need to hear this. After a few more minutes of their babble, I heard the music blast in as they opened the door and left.

Slowly, I changed out of my miniskirt and back into my jeans. Then I sat on the toilet seat and thought about how I'd allowed myself to get to this point. When I began trembling, I put my forehead against the cool metal of the door frame and waited—for the earth to open, for tears, for *something*. But nothing happened.

I inched open the door, saw that the coast was clear, and walked out of the stall. I splashed cold water on my face and stared at myself in the mirror for a long moment as the bass vibrated through the floors and walls of that gray, metal bathroom. Then I went out to the parking lot. I was looking for Stan Ho, the resident Maple Ridge booze dealer.

I'd only had alcohol a couple of times with Cindy—vodka and orange juice. We'd become silly and giggly until it wore off, but each time we'd been closely monitored by either Toni or Mary who made sure we didn't overdo it. However, now seemed like a good time to have a drink, in my mind.

I couldn't go home just yet. Even though I'd become somewhat used to having a separate life outside the home lately, I couldn't bear the thought of pretending that I was okay. I wasn't.

I'd known Stan since fifth grade. His father owned the local liquor store, and Stan nabbed boxes of booze to sell out of the back of his truck. He never got busted because he was too smart for that—he wasn't FSL, but he was an honors student with massive small-business skills.

We had bonded because of our names. Stan had gotten teased even more than me.

I saw his black Explorer in a darkened corner of the parking lot and walked to the open window on the driver's side.

"Hey, Stan."

He looked up, surprised. "Jazz! What's going on?" Then he looked at my eyes. "You okay?"

I nodded. "I want to buy something."

"Yeah?" He raised his eyebrows, but didn't move.

"Yeah," I said, firmly.

He got out, walked to the back of the truck and rifled through a box. "I got J.D., Johnny Walker, Tanqueray, Stoli," he said with a grin. "Name your poison."

I took a deep breath in, mainly to keep my voice from quivering. "Something easy on the taste buds, Stan."

He thought for a moment, then reached into the back. "Schnapps, it is. Peach or peppermint?"

I left Stan's Explorer and went around to the back of the school. I sat down on a step by the back doors and leaned against the wall. I could hear the music thumping through the closed doors as I looked up at the stars. I wondered if Tyler was at Observation Point right now, whispering to another girl to kiss him.

I opened up the bottle of peach schnapps and took a sip. It tasted sweet, almost like a dessert. Stan was right, this stuff was good.

At some point, I realized the bottle was half full and I was dancing by myself to an Akon tune. *"Nobody wanna see us to-ge-ther. . . ."*

Who needed Tyler? And Cindy? And anyone else? He could have his Bubblicious empty calories. Bubblicious, my butt.

That cracked me up—bubblicious, my butt. My butt *was* a bit bubblicious, now that I thought about it.

I pulled out my cell phone and noticed that my mom had tried to call me several times. For some reason this was hilarious to me, too. I erased her messages, and before I knew it, I'd dialed Mit's number.

"Hey, all! You've reached Mit's cell. You know what to do at the sound of the beep!"

I left a long and rambling message, including holding the phone up toward the music so Mit could feel like he was with me.

I drank some more and danced until my hips weren't the only things swaying. I held on to the wall, and walked my hands down until I was sitting again. Everything started whirling around me. I closed my eyes. Bad, bad move.

Next thing I knew, I was spewing chunks all over the pavement. When my stomach was emptied of what felt like everything I'd eaten in the last week, I lay down with my cheek against the ground. I could have heard the galloping of horses twenty miles away.

And then, the voice of God. "Jazz?"

I looked up into the sky. "I'm sorry," I whispered. "I swear I will never, *ever* do this again as long as I live."

"Jazz."

"No, really. I mean it—*never* again."

"Jazz, get up."

Wait a minute. God's voice sounded eerily like Jeevan Sahota's.

He stepped into my line of vision and held his hand out. "Come on, get up," he said. "I was playing ball with the guys, and thought I'd swing by to see who was at the dance."

"Nobody," I said. "Nobody is at that fracking dance."

I reached out, grabbed his hand with both of mine, and held on. He led me out of the school yard, to a bench in the parkette. The same parkette where Tyler gave me my first kiss. I landed on the bench with a thud, noticing briefly that there were a few tomato-colored chunks on my shoes.

Gross.

Jeeves reached into his backpack and pulled out a huge bottle of water. I held my hands out for it. Instead of passing it to me, he dumped half of it over my head.

"What the—?!" I yelled, leaping up.

Bad, *bad* idea. The world lost most of its color as it whipped around me at tornado speed. I reached for the back of the bench and lowered myself down again, gingerly this time.

"It'll help you come out of it," he said matter-of-factly. Then he handed me the rest of the water. "Sip it. *Slowly.*"

I did as he instructed.

We sat there like that for a few moments as I sipped my water. Then, out of nowhere, totally without my permission, a whole bunch of tears slipped down my face. "I thought it was supposed to be simple. You find someone, fall in love, get married, live happily ever after. Isn't that what they told us in kindergarten, Jeeves? It worked for Cinderella and all those princesses. . . . But it's obviously not in the cards for people like me."

I saw Jeeves's leg start jiggling like my dad's did whenever it looked like my mom was going to cry. I looked up, wiped my nose with the back of my hand, then dropped my head back down. "I'm a mess."

"Yeah, you are," he said. He sank down on his knees in front of me and put his hands on my shoulders. He looked directly into my eyes.

"Well, thank you," I said, narrowing my eyes. I pulled my sleeve down and wiped my eyes and nose with the back of it. Then I smoothed back my hair. Like that would make the tomato chunks, raccoon eyes, and nose-water leaking into the corners of my mouth, *way* less noticeable.

"Jazz."

I wished he would stop looking at me like that, like I was too pathetic for words. Which, I admit, at that moment could have been true, but I didn't need *him* to tell me that.

"*What?*" I finally asked.

He dropped his hands, sighed, and heaved himself up onto the bench next to me. We sat there like that for another moment.

Every vein and blood vessel in my brain was swollen, and all I wanted was to check out. I dropped my head onto Jeeves's shoulder and closed my eyes. He leaned his face against the top of my head and sighed again. I could feel him shaking his head for the hundred-millionth time.

I heard his voice as a vibration throughout his body, underneath my cheek. "It *can* work for you. Auntie Kinder and Dr. Babaloo are proof," he said. "Wasn't that the initial point of getting them together? To prove that true love is possible? That dreams can come true and all that crap?"

I lifted my head to look at him through the tears that suddenly sprang into my eyes. I nodded vigorously.

"Come on," he said, standing up and holding out a hand. "Let's get you home."

He walked me all the way home. I thanked him (and silently, God, for my heavy sleeper of a mom). I didn't know what else to say, but I knew there was so much more there. Later. I would figure it out later.

But apparently not. Somehow, in my post-drunkenness, I missed one very crucial detail: all the lights were on in the house as I walked up the steps.

Major Drama in the Dhatt House

Both Dhatt parents are home, waiting for their genius daughter to show up, half-inebriated from a dance she was not supposed to be at.

Enter Jazz Dhatt, FSL student extraordinaire. Her face is flushed, there are chunks of regurgitated dinner all over her hair, clothes, and shoes, lipstick is smeared far around the outline of her lips, eyeliner trails snake down her cheeks. She stumbles in the door to find herself face to face with the Dhatt parents.

Mrs. Dhatt: [mouth drops open as she collapses onto the loveseat.]

Mr. Dhatt: Jassy! WHERE HAVE YOU BEEN?

Jazz: Um. . . .

Mrs. Dhatt: Speak up, Jassy.

Mr. Dhatt: *Kuriye*, these shenanigans of yours shame the family name! Do you know I had to leave work early after a hysterical phone call from your mother? In all the years I have been working, not once has anything like this ever happened!

Jazz: [is completely alert now]

Mrs. Dhatt: [Sounding tired] Maybe there's a nice convent school we can find for Jassy in India, *heh-na*? They might have better luck straightening her out.

Mr. Dhatt: We didn't know if you were in a ditch somewhere, or if someone had—

Jazz: A convent school?

Mrs. Dhatt: Look, she's playing dumb. How dare you make fools out of us!

Jazz: But, wait. . . .

Mrs. Dhatt: Wait? *Wait?* "Wait," she says!

Mr. Dhatt: Enough. You did this to yourself, Jassy.

I would have preferred yelling and hysterics to the deadly calm I got. I could see it in their eyes—how deeply disappointed they were in me. And I couldn't blame them one bit. I knew I'd broken something that couldn't be unbroken.

Chapter 20

After the night of the dance, the parental third degree in my house reached unprecedented proportions. I wouldn't have put it past my parents to hire detectives to follow me around; they were that angry.

I told Mit about what happened and he laughed for a solid three minutes—I checked my watch. "It is NOT funny," I growled.

"It kinda is, Jazzy," he said gasping for breath. When he finally sobered up, he said, "At least they didn't kick you out of the house and disown you."

"They might as well have," I said. But I knew it wasn't the same. My parents hadn't said I was "dead" to them—and somewhere underneath all that anger, I knew they still loved me.

"I'm sorry, Mit. I know it's not the same. . . ."

"No, it's okay. I'm not comparing—just saying. You know as well as I do, that some Punjabi girls who, if they got caught doing what you did, would be *exactly* where I am right now—kicked out with no place to go. Even worse, maybe."

I swallowed hard. He was right. I'd grown up hearing cautionary tales of such girls. Clearly all those cautionary tales had done me a lot of good.

After a moment, he said, "I got your message. Sorry I wasn't there that night to tele-hold your hand."

"It's okay. Thanks, anyway. I'm sorry I went lame and psycho on you."

"It wasn't lame and psycho," he said. "Just drunk."

And then he burst into another fit of uncontrollable laughter.

I finally saw Tyler at school. He steadily ignored me until one day he just never came back. I heard one of the bindi-bos saying that he'd been kicked out, but she was the same one who'd said he was rich and from Wendell Academy—which I now knew was utter dung. I heard Mandy Morgan, whose mom worked in the school office, say that he'd really just transferred from some school in another zone because he was caught cutting too many classes and smoking on school property.

Cindy and I had a serious BFF-to-BFF chat about everything, and she was my total BFF again. It went something like this:

Me: Cin, I was a butt-wipe.

Her: Yes.

Me: If I ever do anything that stupid again, feel free to call me whatever names you think appropriate.

Her: I will. [Pause] Jazz, I know I could never understand you and your life, but I'm your best friend and I care about you. And my job is to make sure *you* care about you, too.

Me: [Sniffling] I know.

Her: [Quietly] I'll never know what it's like to be you, Jazz. Just like you'll never know what it's like to have a single mom and a dad who started over with a brand new family on another continent. But if I ever did something stupid, I'd want you to tell me the truth.

Me: [Giving her biggest, squeeziest hug in history] I totally will.

And that was that.

Another good thing was that Jeeves was talking to me again. He said he'd given up on me until the night of the dance—"Then, I realized you just couldn't live without me."

For that, he got a nice whack to the shoulder with my backpack.

But I was happy to be walking home with him again. Even though most of our walks were in silence, it wasn't uncomfortable silence.

Today, it was just us, because Cindy and Wes were off doing their Cin-Wes-ery.

"Wait," I said, stopping at a playground and walking to a swing. I pushed off and swung myself as high as I could go.

Jeeves jumped on the swing next to me. "You're still lame on the swings, Dhatt."

I grinned, remembering our childhood swing races. "Up yours, Sahota."

He pumped until his swing started bumping, then jumped off.

"Holy crud! You're going to break something, you doofus!" I yelled.

He brushed himself off and smiled. "Chicken turd."

I let my swing slow down a bit, then sailed through the air.

Bad move. "OWWWWW!!!"

"Jazz! You all right?" He was immediately by my side, holding my ankle in one hand and poking it with the other. "Does this hurt?"

"AAAAAIIIIIIYYYYYY-YES!!!"

"And this?"

"OUCH!! YES."

"Good. You're going to be fine. It's just a sprain."

"Ow! See what you did?"

He laughed. "What *I* did?"

"Yes, you dingo. This is all your fault!"

He chuckled again and helped me limp to a nearby bench. "Here," he said, "stick with something more your speed, *behbeh*."

I punched him on the shoulder for calling me an old lady. "*Behbeh?!* You're lucky I have a sprained ankle!"

He smiled. "It's nice to see you again, Jazz."

I looked back at him for a moment and knew what he meant. It had been ages since I felt this way. Like I was me again, the Jazz

I always knew myself to be. I got a lump in my throat as I watched him turn and walk to the climbers.

He climbed up and slid down the pole, then climbed the rope-webby thing as I massaged my ankle. He was right, my ankle was already starting to feel better. I put my foot on the ground to test it. Huh, almost good as new.

Jeeves did a backward flip-thingy off one of the climbers and landed on his feet a few feet away from me. For just a split second, I caught another glimpse of what all the fuss was about—why the bindi-bos got their thongs all bunched up when LL Cool Jeeves was around.

His hair was long enough to fall into his eyes, so he was always flicking it back. He was nimble on the basketball courts and his joints all seemed loose and oiled when he moved. Even though every time I looked at him I saw a geeky new kid, the chest I was staring at right this minute had nothing to do with any kind of geekiness.

He was breathing heavy from his jungle-gym acrobatics, with a goofy grin punctuated by two dimples on either cheek.

He stared at me for a moment, then shoved his hands into his pockets. "What's up, Jazz?" he asked quietly.

"Huh?"

"Where are you?"

"Oh." I felt my face grow warm.

He leaned against the orange, igloo-shaped climber.

Before I knew what was happening, I was standing mere millimeters from his chest. His breath came out in little puffs, leaving damp circles on my forehead.

"Jazz."

I stretched up on my toes, holding on to his shoulders and grazed my mouth against his. Whisper soft. I closed my eyes, brushed my forehead against his dimpled cheek and looked up into his eyes.

He didn't kiss me back, or make any move to reciprocate. Just stood there stiffly, watching my face. We stood like that for something like an hour before I slowly morphed into my dork alter ego.

"I think you're confused, Dhatt," he said quietly.

Those quiet words hit me like a million bee stings. Jeeves was totally right—he should not be my consolation prize for losing Tyler.

I sank to my heels and dropped my head. "I have to figure some things out," I said.

He grasped my upper arms and firmly, but gently, pushed me back one step. He reached down to grab both our backpacks and said, "Yup. Let's go home. I gotta take a piss."

He'll never know how eternally grateful I was for those words.

When we reached his house, I took his hand. "Jeeves," I said, looking up into his eyes. "I'm sorry about that. . . ."

He looked at the ground. "It's cool."

I let go of his hand and took my backpack from him.

"Listen, Jazz," he said, shoving his hands into his pockets. "I don't know what's going on, but. . . ."

I gave him a small smile. "It's cool," I said, walking up the street to my house.

When I got home, my mom said—in the short, efficient sentences she and my dad used with me these days—that she had to step out to grab a few things for the eggplant dish we were having that night.

I dropped my stuff on my bed, then thought it might be nice to study outside on the front porch. I pulled out my homework and set myself up in a shady spot. I focused on equations for a while until I heard a car pull in. My mom hadn't taken the car, so I looked up, expecting someone who had made a wrong turn and was probably backing up already.

Instead, I saw the familiar shape and color of Tyler's enormous car. The same one I had made out in numerous times over the past couple of months. With a horrendous thudding in my ears and utter chaos in my belly, I closed my book and put my pencil down.

"Hey, Baby J.," he said, striding up our front walk.

Just like that. *Hey, Baby J.* Like I'd just seen him yesterday and everything was totally fine.

I could barely breathe. I wanted to ask him where he'd been and why he hadn't called or texted, and a million other questions. But I felt like that would open up parts of me that I'd finally managed to find some peace with. I didn't want to wake them again and lose myself like I had in the past couple of months.

So, I just said, "Hi. What are you doing here?"

"I was driving by and saw you. Thought I'd stop and. . . ." he trailed off, then brought his hand around from behind his back. There was a perfect, saffron-colored marigold in it and he held it out to me. "Listen, I'm sorry about everything."

I said nothing. I couldn't. If I'd opened my mouth, I probably would've started crying, and that would not have been pretty.

He shifted his weight to the other foot. "I know it might not seem like it, but I really like you."

I nodded. "You could've fooled me," I said quietly.

He faced me. "I got so much crap going on, Jazz," he said. I saw the play of shadows on his face for just a split second before he covered them up again. "I turn eighteen next month and I'm trying to find ways to legally adopt my sister and get her out of the house. I don't want her there with my dad."

My heart twisted as I remembered Sianna's round, dark eyes. Then images of Mr. R. flashed across my mind. And I thought about Auntie Kinder's legal battles. "That's not going to be easy."

He laughed bitterly. "It's going to be damn near impossible." He looked off to the side. "But I'm still going to try. I can't live there anymore. But I can't leave Sianna there without me."

"I wish I could help," I said softly. I really meant it. I could see the sadness in his eyes, and I knew how hard it was to see people you loved being mistreated—and wanting to help, but knowing there's only so much you could do.

Kind of the way I'd felt about him, maybe, the day I'd met his parents.

He looked into my eyes. "I know you do. What you went through with your aunt and uncle told me a lot. You're good people, Jazz."

Then why were you making out with every girl this side of the Equator? I bit my lip.

"That's why I had to come by. I wanted to call a truce."

I worked to regulate my breathing. "Isn't a truce for war time?"

He smiled. "I guess. I don't remember what we're warring about, but. . . ."

Um, that you did IT with Bubblicious?

Part of me wanted to slap the snot out of him, and the other part of me wanted to gleefully jump into his arms and lick him all over like a puppy.

He stuck his hand out. "Truce?"

"Truce," I said, my voice coming out all gravelly. The contact made everything sizzle inside me. *Tssssssss.*

He looked around. "Are you alone?"

I nodded.

"Can I come inside?"

Uh, NO. "Are you insane? My mother would kill me. Plus, I'm trying to make up for annihilating any trust they ever placed in me."

He nodded and stepped back. "Can I use your bathroom?"

The thought of my mother coming home to find me with a strange boy in our house filled me with a kind of terror you can not imagine. "No."

He widened his eyes. "I can't even use the bathroom?"

I shook my head.

"Wow. Your parents *are* strict." He stood looking at me for another moment. "Can I have a hug, then? Just for old times' sake?"

And that's how my mother found us. Me and Tyler, standing on my front porch, with our arms wrapped around one another.

Chapter 21

"Jassy! What is the meaning of this? And in front of our house for all the world to see and mock? You, boy! Go on from here! Shame, shame! INSIDE, Jassy! NOW."

I was on complete lockdown house arrest until we left for India. That meant doing everything around the house that my parents didn't feel like doing. I cleaned out the refrigerator, cleaned out all the kitchen cabinets, the tiles around the bathtub, the car, steam-cleaned the basement. . . . Shall I go on?

Good thing number one: I found out from Auntie Kinder that my parents only intended to scare me with this trip. Once they simmered down from their red-hot rage, they'd decided the trip would only be for the summer, but they weren't going to let me know that.

When I asked Auntie Kinder why she told me, she stroked my cheek and said, "You've been through plenty enough, love."

Good thing number two: Auntie Kinder and Pammi were finally rid of the former Mr. Auntie Kinder—at least for now. Dr.

Babaloo got his team of London lawyers involved immediately. A couple of official letters from the Law Offices of Blackwell & Yardsley later, Mr. Jackass agreed to stay away from both of them, no issues at all. I remembered my mom's comment that some men only took the word of other men seriously. I wondered whose word it would take to keep Mr. R. away from Sianna and Tyler. Whoever's it was, I hoped Tyler would find it.

Good thing number three: I finally talked to Mit again.

"Josh and I are moving in together."

"Wow, Mit—that's serious!"

His voice was vibrating with excitement. "It *is*. He's totally my soul mate, Jazzy! And his parents have kind of, like, adopted me. They're Hawaiian—Hawaii has this amazing history and spirit of resistance . . . . Anyway, his parents have a whole different take on everything. They've always accepted that Josh is gay. . . . Oh, Jazzy, I think things are going to be okay!"

I felt tears spring to my eyes. "I'm so happy for you! You totally deserve it."

"Thanks, Jazzy," he said, sounding pleased. Then in a more serious voice, "I'm sorry things didn't work out with buttface Tyler. Or should I be glad?"

I sighed. "He's actually not as butt-faced as I thought. He's got a whole lot of crap to deal with just like us. But you're right, it's just so hard, you know?"

"Tell me about it." His voice went quiet. "I still think about my parents and the whole 'family' thing, I feel like the gash inside me is as fresh as the day it happened."

I swallowed the pit in my throat. "Maybe they'll come around?" I said, wondering if I was saying it about my own parents as much as his.

As if reading my mind, he drew a deep breath and said, "Maybe yours, Jazzy. But mine? Not likely."

"Thanks for coming clean with my parents."

"Well, once that journalist snapped all those pictures of me on Pride Day and plastered them all over the front page of the local paper, I figured I could help you out a little."

I giggled, remembering the images Mit had emailed her. "You two looked awesome in your coordinated outfits."

"You ain't seen nothin' honey," he said laughing. It was a good sound to hear.

When we hung up, I thought about the fact that my parents never really meant to "ship" me off to India the way they'd always threatened to. In my mind, I had concocted whole scenarios of what that might mean. Instead, they were basically giving me a two month time-out to get me away from what they thought were bad influences. And to connect me with what was important to them, way down into their cores.

So here I was, a few weeks before our flight to the Motherland, mowing our lawn and pulling the farcking weeds out by hand. My parents might not be as enraged as they had been, but they were ruthless, nonetheless.

And, even though Mit came out to them, they stuck to their story—that I was a big, fat, deceiving LIAR. And for the past couple of months, I had been exactly that.

Auntie Kinder told my mom about Tyler (though not *everything*, thank God) and my mom said, "Jassy, if you had told us there was a nice, Indian boy you liked and brought him by the house to meet us, it wouldn't have been as unforgivable. But *this*, this lying and sneaking around. . . ? Absolutely unacceptable!"

I knew that wasn't true. Even if I had come home and said I wanted to marry Jeeves—who was Punjabi and Indian and Sikh, but not the same caste—there would still have been problems. Maybe not the huge problems that came with dating a guy like Tyler, but problems, nonetheless.

I bent over to wrestle with another dandelion when I heard the clinking of ice in a glass behind me. I turned around to see Jeeves walking up the drive with a tall glass of lemonade. I snatched it from his hand and downed it in a nanosecond.

"You're welcome, Rude."

I made a sour face. "This lemonade sucks, Sahota."

"I'll tell my mom you think so."

I smacked his arm and sat down on the curb for a breather. "What d'you want? I got a whole yard to weed and hedges to trim."

He sat down next to me. "So you're off to India."

I nodded, putting the cold glass to my forehead. I'd worked up quite a sweat with all that mowing and weeding.

"For how long?"

I shrugged. "They won't tell me. But I know they want me back in time for school in September. Principal Steinke said I could use these next few weeks to make up for what I screwed up this semester."

He picked up a stone and flung it. "Lucky. But you might not be able to make up everything."

I looked at him, then down at the ground. "What do you mean by that?"

He was quiet for a moment. "Some things you can't make up."

"Jeeves, I apologized for that day in the playground. I was a moron—"

"I wasn't talking about that," he said, waving my words away. "Actually, I didn't mind *that* at all."

I gave him a look.

He grinned and shrugged. "Hey, I'm a guy, you mauled me . . . what do you want?"

"I did not *maul* you, Sahota. . . . In your dreams."

"I meant you still owe me two study weekends. Don't think I've forgotten Dhatt. You got debts."

I groaned. "Oh, no—Latin! I'd totally forgotten."

"I didn't. I won, fair and square," he said with a grin.

"Yeah, whatever," I said, and stuck my tongue out.

He looked like he was about to say something else, but thought better of it. Instead, he picked up another stone and examined it. "Do your parents have a Guided Dating Plan for you in India?"

My gut wrenched. "They said they wouldn't."

"You believe them?"

I inhaled deeply and exhaled. "No. But they spent a lot of time talking to Dr. Babaloo and Auntie Kinder—I have to have faith in that."

He nodded and watched a car drive by. When it was gone, he stared at the corner where it had been before it turned. "What do girls see in that guy, anyway?"

"Tyler?" My heart flipped as I said his name out loud.

He nodded, staring out at the street.

I thought for a moment. "He kind of . . . made it easy for me to do things I wouldn't normally do, I guess."

He looked at the ground and picked up another stone. "Things you wouldn't do with, say . . . a guy like me."

I looked away, into the hedge between our house and the neighbor's. Jeeves had been my friend and playmate since we were kids. He knew me better than any other guy in the world, other than my dad—and even then, Jeeves knew things about me that, thank all the deities, my dad would never know. I could count on Jeeves in ways that I didn't even count on Cindy. Why, oh, why could I not just fall in love with him, dear godz?

But I didn't want Jeeves. I wanted Tyler, in all his mess and complexity and anguish and sweetness and hotness. I liked the way my heart pounded and my stomach twisted when I was with him. I didn't feel like that with Jeeves. I felt loved and liked and safe. Warm, not hot. With Tyler, I was on a tightrope miles and miles above the ground, so close I could touch the stars. With Jeeves, I would never fall.

But I knew that Tyler was the type of guy who could keep "unintentionally" hurting people he loved—and truly not mean to, even. Did I want to keep being on the receiving end of that? I didn't know—I didn't think so. It didn't feel very good, no matter how awesome the other person was. But I knew one thing for sure—I wouldn't have learned that about myself if I hadn't met Tyler and followed my heart. And I wouldn't have known that Jeeves didn't set my insides quivering like Tyler could if I hadn't taken some of those risks.

Were they worth it?

Again, I didn't know. I'd lost my parents' trust and disappointed them in some pretty major ways. But whatever I'd broken needed to be broken. It wasn't real. Now, my parents saw the *true* me—a combination of Jazz and Jassy and Jazzy and Baby J.—not the ideal Jassy they'd etched in their minds. What was broken could heal. Differently, but stronger.

I thought, with some sadness, of Mit. He'd taken a lot of the same risks that I had, but his parents had turned their backs on him.

It wasn't fair, but at least he was happy. He was being himself now, in a home where that was not only okay, it was cherished.

Was I too busy looking for the giant, all-consuming love I'd read about; the one that woke sleeping beauties out of eternal sleep and whisked lovely maidens away from their wicked stepmothers, transforming them into princesses in glittering ball gowns? A love that sent my heart racing and made my tongue go numb; that made an FSL—Future Star and Leader—student like me do stupid things despite knowing better?

I swallowed hard. What if Love wasn't all that? What if it was quieter, like a whisper on a breeze that you had to listen real hard for? Or smaller, like a cardamom seed that's soothing and pungent and explosive all at once? What if it was this . . . something as simple as a cold glass of lemonade on a sweltering afternoon?

I set the glass I had been cradling down between us; the glass of lemonade that he, Jeevan Sahota, had brought down the block for me. "No," I said, propping my face up on one fist so that I could look at him. "I never would have done those things with you, Jeeves."

He shot the stone out into the street.

"That's a good thing." I reached over to lay a hand on his arm.

He took it in one of his, swallowing my entire hand in his gargantuan, basketball-palming ones. He picked up the glass with the other.

He smiled. "Looking forward to your trip?"

I sighed. "Not really. I'm nervous. What if I get sick?"

"Count on it. Every time we go, I get either diarrhea or constipation, or swing back and forth between the two. But the food is awesome. Just boil the water at least ten minutes before you drink it."

"Lovely."

He grinned. "Get ready for beggars and squat-toilets, baby. And you think *this* is hot? Just wait."

I wasn't sure whether I should leave my hand in Jeeves's or move it away. Leaving it there might give him the wrong idea, but I liked having it there. It was familiar . . . comforting.

We sat there for a few moments longer, with me debating the hand issue and not doing anything about it.

He let go of my hand held his arms out. "I'll see you when you get back."

"I'll see you when I get back," I said, hugging him warmly, and being careful to make it a very clearly *friendly* hug, complete with some back-patting.

When he left, I watched him walk all the way to his house before I turned to walk up the steps into mine. I wondered if that was what my parents had. Did they start out becoming friends, then more? Or did they get thrown into a marriage, start having kids, then slowly got to know one another?

I realized how little I knew about anything related to love. I'd groped along, looking for clues and answers, and found myself under a giant heap of more questions. But at least I knew what the questions were now. That's more than I knew before I met Tyler.

Now, in a few weeks, I was leaving for my first trip to India, with parents who were quite possibly on the lookout for my life partner. My father had said that this trip was to help me "reconnect with my roots." To take me back to the soil where my parents' parents and their parents' parents had grown and lived and struggled and died.

And, even though she was still angry, my mother assured me that this trip in no way had anything to do with finding me a life partner. This sounded suspiciously rehearsed, like something she came up with after one of the many long conversations with Dr. Babaloo and Auntie Kinder, but I hoped it was true.

Auntie Kinder had finally found her "fellow," and Pammi was coming around fast, now that she knew he really was as great as he seemed. And best of all, an American television producer, a friend of Roger's, was interested in creating an American version of Dr. Babaloo's show for cable, so Dr. Babaloo had begun the process of relocating to New York City.

The thought of Tyler could still get my heart beating like it was getting ready to shoot to the moon, but I wouldn't see him for a couple of months. That was probably a good thing. And for better or for worse, my parents got a glimpse of me in a different light, maybe closer to who I really was as opposed to who they wanted me to be.

I didn't know what was going to happen next. But whatever it was, I, Baby J., a.k.a. Jasbir Dhatt, was ready.

Bring it.

~ ❋ ~

About the Author

Born in a rural Punjabi village (with no running water and electricity!), Neesha Meminger grew up in Toronto, Canada, and now lives and works in the mega urban metropolis of New York City. She writes stories of strong girls and women, and the people they love.

Neesha's first novel, *SHINE, COCONUT MOON*, made the Smithsonian's list of Notable Books for Children in its debut year and was listed on the New York Public Library's *Stuff for the Teen Age—Top 100 Books for Teens*. The book was also nominated for the American Library Association's *Best Books for Young Adults*, and for the online CYBILS award. *JAZZ IN LOVE* is Neesha's second novel.

~ ❋ ~

For more information, visit NeeshaMeminger.com
On Facebook as Neesha Meminger
On Twitter: @NeeshaMem

Sample *JAZZ IN LOVE* Discussion Guide
for Educators and Book Clubs
For a Complete Discussion Guide, Visit NeeshaMeminger.com

Sample Discussion Questions

1. Jazz describes her parents as super-strict. What might they be trying to protect by monitoring their daughter so closely?

2. At several points in the novel, Jazz talks about not feeling "Indian enough." What does she mean by this? Are there areas in your life where you feel not "something" enough? What makes you feel this way?

3. What does meeting Tyler's parents tell Jazz about him and his life? What is he struggling with? Do you see any similarities between his struggles and Pammi and Auntie Kinder's?

4. How does Jazz excuse some of Tyler's behavior? Would you excuse this type of behavior in someone you were interested in? Why or why not?

5. Auntie Kinder is of the same generation as Jazz's parents. Why do you think she is less traditional than they are?

Sample Activities and Writing Exercises

1.   Throughout the novel, we learn that arranged marriages were once common in Britain and other parts of Europe. Do some research to find out why the practice was eventually phased out, or grew out of fashion, and write a one-page summary of your findings.

2.   Set up a debate in your classroom, book club, or group with two teams. Have one side take a pro-arranged marriage stance and the other side against. You might want to use a point system to keep score, or you might decide who wins by determining which team manages to sway the other team's opinion.

3.   Write a scene from Cindy's, Pammi's, or Jeeves's perpective. Think about how they would view Jazz and her decisions. Do they approve? Do they try to stop her?

For downloadable discussion questions, activities and writing exercises, visit NeeshaMeminger.com

Also by Neesha Meminger:

Shine, Coconut Moon

Praise for *Shine, Coconut Moon*

"This novel takes a hard look at diversity, friendship, family, prejudice, tolerance, misunderstanding, ignorance, and terrorism, culminating in what it means to 'know thyself.' The book handles

these issues nicely by telling the story of a compelling and likeable character trying to find her real identity. It is an enjoyable, difficult-to-put-down book. Readers will learn about a unique religion and culture and how it can feel for minorities living and assimilating into American life after September 11."
—*VOYA*, June, 2009

"This straightforward and ultimately reassuring novel reads like an older Sikh version of *Are You There God? It's Me, Margaret* and will fill a niche in any school or public library looking to beef up their YA multicultural fiction offerings."
—*Kirkus Reviews*, February, 2009

"This novel is especially poignant as our country continues to deal with prejudice against [South] Asians and individuals from the Middle East. Readers will be drawn in to Sam's story and her struggles to make sense of and combine her two cultures. This admirably explores identity and difference through the voice of a girl . . . [who] is a 'typical' teenager."
—*Booklist*, February, 2009

"Meminger's book is a beautiful and sensitive portrait of a young woman's journey from self-absorbed naivete to selfless, unified awareness."
—*School Library Journal*, 2009

CPSIA information can be obtained
at www.ICGtesting.com
Printed in the USA
BVOW08s2310281017
498929BV00001B/25/P